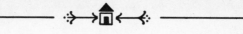

# HOME

## GOD'S DESIGN

## Celebrating a Sense of Place

*by Miriam Huffman Rockness*

Zondervan Books
Zondervan Publishing House
Grand Rapids, Michigan

Home: God's Design
Celebrating a Sense of Place
Copyright © 1990 by Miriam Huffman Rockness

Zondervan Books are published by
Zondervan Publishing House
1415 Lake Drive, S.E.,
Grand Rapids, Michigan 49506

Library of Congress Cataloging-in-Publication Data

Rockness, Miriam Huffman. 1944–
    Home, God's design : celebrating a sense of place / Miriam Huffman
Rockness.
        c.  pm.
    ISBN 0-310-59081-7
    1. Architectures Domestic—Psychological aspects.
    2. Architecture and society. 3. Home. 4. Rockness, Miriam Huffman,
    1944–  —Homes and haunts. I. Title.
    NA7125.R55  1990
    728'.01—dc20                                                90–39750
                                                                      CIP

*Edited by Evelyn Bence*

*Printed in the United States of America*

90  91  92  93  94  95  96  97 / AK / 10  9  8  7  6  5  4  3  2  1

*Lovingly dedicated*
*to my parents,*
*John and Dorothy Huffman,*
*who, in giving me a home*
*in the deepest sense of the word,*
*provided a blueprint*
*to adapt to the requirements*
*of my own family unit*

*A house is built of logs and stone,*
*Of tiles and posts and piers:*
*A home is built of loving deeds*
*That stand a thousand years.*
—*Victor Hugo*

# ACKNOWLEDGMENTS

I want to thank Evelyn Bence, whose unfailing encouragement and priceless editorial skills have been indispensable to the writing of this book. Once again I thank Milford Myhre, who muddled through the early draft, pressing me to clarify my thoughts with the continual challenge: "I know what you meant, but it's not what you said."

Essential to writing are places of solitude. For making available such places, I'm indebted to Emily Schoenhofen; Robin Gibson and his supportive staff at the law firm of Gibson and Lilly; and Jonathan Shaw and his staff at Bok Tower Gardens.

Finally, I'm deeply grateful to my husband and children, who permitted me to open the doors of our home through the pages of this book and who gave loving support throughout the writing process.

# TABLE OF CONTENTS

Introduction  15

Prologue: What Is Home?  19

Chapter 1 / Foundations: "Build Sure in the
    Beginning"  25
    Deeper than Remembrance  27
    Delightful My Inheritance  31
    Places of the Heart  37
    The Beauty of the House  42
    Agreeable Hours  46
    Garret Gallery  50
    The Cornerstone of Truth  57

Chapter 2 / Roof and Exterior Walls:
    Sheltering Elements  61
    A Shelter in the Time of Storm  63
    The Bond of Family  67
    The Grace of Courtesy  72
    Open Doors to Communication  77
    A Time to Celebrate  81
    Reaching Out  86

Chapter 3 / Walls: Delineation of
    Space and Place  91
    Resonance of Rooms  93
    A Room of One's Own  98
    Hub of the House  102

The Nest     **106**
Salute to the Old-Fashioned Front Porch     **109**
Two Solitudes: One Solidarity     **113**
More than Dining     **117**

**Chapter 4 / Elements of Style:**
**Decoration and Design     121**
What Is Style?     **123**
Developing a Personal Style     **128**
A Joy Forever     **133**
A Time to Grow     **137**
My Favorite Things     **141**
All Good Gifts     **145**

**Chapter 5 / Doors and Thresholds:**
**The Open Door of Hospitality     151**
The Glory of the House Is Hospitality     **153**
A Sheltering Hood     **157**
A Portion of Oneself     **161**
Company's Coming!     **166**
The Pleasure of Their Company     **171**
Guise of a Stranger     **176**

**Chapter 6 / Window-Songs:**
**A Personal View     181**
View from My Window     **183**
Burden of Liberty     **186**
Belle Lettres     **191**
Windows of the Mind     **195**
Icon Corner     **201**
Through Eyes of Faith     **204**

**Chapter 7 / The Road by My Door:**
**Growing Up to Go Away     209**
The Road Leads On     **211**

Soliloquy on a Sleeping Boy    216
An Open Letter to Kimberly    218
The Birds and the Bees    224
Growing Pains    228
Lead Them Safely Home    233
All Other Ground    237

**Epilogue**
Land of Heart's Desire    245

# INTRODUCTION

A decade has passed since I wrote about my adjustments to motherhood, trying to set up a household when I was more than a thousand miles from the place I considered "home." *Keep These Things* was the result of frantic scribblings, jotted during chinks of time salvaged from my obligations to a baby, a toddler, a grade-schooler, and my young husband, adjusting to demands of his new parish ministry. I turned to writing in a desperate effort to make order out of chaos, sense out of confusion.

Now, again I turn to paper to process the particulars of my life situation. Significant changes have transpired since those first years in Lake Wales, Florida. My three children are all in school, giving me thirty free hours a week to use or squander to my choosing. We have moved from our "Best Nest," a snug wooden bungalow, to the opposite side of the street. Our "House of Houses" is a spacious two-story, white-frame structure that all but shouts "home": a sprawling wrap-around porch, window boxes spilling with greenery, and a bright red door of welcome. Furthermore, I've undergone a significant change of heart: I now respond to people as friends, not strangers, and to this place, once so foreign, as home.

While my earlier years were marked by transition and adjustment, I am now undergirded by a fundamental stability that comes from developing a strong sense of place and a growing understanding of my role in the scheme of things. My children's lives, in contrast to their unpredictable younger years, are clearly defined by their school schedules and extracurricular activities. No longer need I snatch moments in which to write; I can reserve several quiet mornings each week for extended writing.

Rather than the constant physical presence of children, I'm shadowed by the disturbing reality that my children are growing up—and growing away. David, a "rising" high school junior, is a tall broad-shouldered fellow whose deep voice continues to startle me, as it so closely resembles the resonant sound of his father. Eighth-grader Kimberly hovers between girl and woman, something poignantly shown by her growing desire to see her dolls as part of the decor rather than as playmates. Only ten-year-old Jonathan retains total claim to childhood. Yet even he hurries through this precious stage, always pressing to keep up with his older siblings. How I savor the time that remains for me in their busy schedules.

Indeed, it was this very consciousness of limited time that produced the tension that gave impetus to this book. The importance of each moment was magnified as I realized that time was running out—sand sifting through the narrow neck of an hourglass. Few are the years remaining for me to nurture impressionable young spirits, to instill lasting values in forming characters, and to inculcate a comprehensive worldview in supple minds.

Changing life-situations create new challenges. Our focus is gradually shifting from the social concerns of childhood shyness and sharing to adolescent challenges of peer pressure and standards in dating, from safety concerns of supervised play to unsupervised driving. I must recognize if not resolve new tensions: How do I structure a home environment that nurtures both a teenage boy and his ten-year-old roommate? How do I encourage independent forays into the outside world and still foster a strong family unit? How do I reconcile my various roles of wife, mother, friend, citizen, writer? How do I balance my enjoyment of the creative aspects of homemaking with my newly acquired freedom to taste and test options beyond the four walls of home?

In these pages I will address these challenges and other questions in the context of daily living. Though the particulars of our family situation are unique, the necessity of and desire for a stable home are universal, as are principles for creating such a haven.

I have used the metaphor *house* to try to capture the elusive essence of *home*.

*Home: God's Design* is an offering of the wood, brick, paint, furnishings, and accessories that literally and figuratively constitute home for us. It is as personal and specific in design and character as the structure in which we live. While my prologue addresses the universal question "What Is Home?" the subsequent reflections reveal one woman's effort to create such a home for her own family. I open the door to others in the belief that others face similar "building" problems in their particular places and that certain principles of design and construction are fundamental to achieving any home anywhere.

So please overlook the slanting floorboards, the chipped paint, and the falling plaster: Welcome to our place!

# PROLOGUE: WHAT IS HOME?

*Home*. What a strangely compelling word, evoking images and sensations of people and places, of time past and time present. For most people *home* denotes a place of safety: It promises shelter from the elements, protection from dangers beyond its exterior walls and roof. *Home* suggests a place of comfort and well-being: a place of unconditional acceptance and belonging where, as Robert Frost wrote, "When you have to go there, they have to take you in."

The powerful pull of home transcends logic. Longings for home are often rooted in a particular place. The lyrics of a Hungarian immigrant song poignantly convey the yearning for one's place of birth. The immigrants longed to return to their village, "where every blade of grass understood Hungarian."[1] Some people find home only by leaving their birthplace to discover a location where they inexplicably feel they belong.

A particular house, perhaps from early childhood, might become the standard by which one measures all other homes. English novelist Elizabeth Goudge refers to her home in Ely as "the home of all homes." She continues, "I have had five homes, all of them lovely, but Ely is the mother-figure."[2] One English friend considers his parents' address, Hayes' Meadow, synonymous with home. He, his brothers, and sister link the name *Hayes* to their own abodes throughout the world: San Francisco-Hayes, Saint James's-Hayes, Culver-Hayes.

19

Unfortunately, the word *home* for some elicits a wistful yearning for something they've never had—an elusive shangri-la. So strong is this sense of home on human psyche that, according to Swiss psychologist Paul Tournier, "homelessness" in the early years can produce lifelong ramifications, an increasingly unsatisfied nostalgia: ever-seeking, never-finding.

Gladys Hunt has related an incident that speaks to this point. As a guest lecturer at a Michigan State University class on family living, she stood in front of her audience with trepidation. Young faces stared forward, expressing emotions ranging from faintly masked boredom to open hostility. Several students straddling windowsills even turned their backs to her. A few conversations continued without so much as a glance her way. One student feigned sleep. Gladys's fear mounted: What could an author-homemaker possibly say that would have relevance to this resistant group?

Breathing deeply, she began to speak in clear, measured syllables: "Home is a safe place." Nothing could have prepared her for their dramatic response to these words. Instantly students straightened to attention. A sustained interest continued throughout the class, while she spoke simply and directly about the value of home. After the bell rang, students crowded around the podium. One after another each expressed a variation of one theme: a longing for a safe place; the failure to find such a place within family or close friendships; ever-seeking, never-finding.

The very word *home* arouses universal nostalgic longings—an ache that can spur a quest for some elusive refuge if not an attempt to revisit or re-create a place past. In reality, places, like relationships, change. Things are in a constant state of flux. Rare is the person who hasn't at some time asked with a sigh, "Where is home?"

That was my question after our move from a familiar region of Illinois and Michigan to semitropical Florida. Far from things familiar and without time to have sunk new roots, I was in an emotional no-man's-land. Even places I have called home—the Cape Cod cottage of my childhood, the ranch-style house of my youth, and the simple apartments of my early married years—were now occupied by strangers and no longer way stations to which I could return. An overwhelming sense of placelessness engulfed me.

Yet I could not indulge this emotion for long. More practical considerations called for my immediate attention: my ever-present toddler, the baby I was expecting, and my husband's adjustment to a challenging new job. This place, despite my feelings, was "our" place. The time had come for "our place," wherever it was, to become "home." My question, "Where is home?" was replaced by two others: "What is home?" and "How can I create that home for my family and myself?"

Fourteen years have since transpired. I can no more fix the moment when this place became home than I can identify instants of growth in my children. Surely tracings along the way mark advances in my heart. But, more than by any incident or given point in time, the transformation of house into home was a culmination of many events, great and small: daily routines, common meals, the comings and goings of family members, shared tears and joys, the benediction of old and new friends, holiday and celebrations—day after day, year after year. To paraphrase Edgar Guest: It takes a heap of living to make a house a home.

The passing of time has brought inevitable changes to our family. Home is less and less the center of activity for

21

our family but more and more a base from which other activities are launched.

Invariably certain questions taunt me: What does home mean to five people spending ever-increasing amounts of time outside its four walls? How important is my presence at home? Indeed, am I *needed* there at all? How important is home at this stage in our family life?

When I listen to whispers from my past and present voices, when I hear my children's present voices and future intimations, I hear an answer: Home provides a quiet center, a unifying base for individuals with diverse pursuits. It helps to form our identity, both as a family and as individuals, by building values, beliefs, and traditions. Within the relative safety of the home, family members forge meaningful human relationships and discover their personal strengths and weaknesses. A secure home enables all of us to find with greater ease our place in an insecure world. Yes, time brings changes. Details and particulars of family life change. But the same big questions remain: What is home? How can I best create that home for myself and for my family?

So I look into my heart and write, realizing only too well that I do not possess definitive answers. I am a fellow learner. No one can duplicate another's experience; each home must be hewn from the raw materials of one's own life. Despite these differences, we parents do have much in common. The particulars vary but the process is similar. So I share my experiences in the hope that it may encourage others.

"You can't go home again," declared novelist Thomas Wolfe. My spirit resists, knowing all the while that his words are in a sense true. We can't go back to homes or places and expect to find them unchanged. But we can take our yearnings for a particular home, real or imagined, and recast them into blueprints for present use. If we cannot return to time past, we can nevertheless salvage certain elements from it and incorporate them into our working drawings for today.

A homemaker is to a home what an architect is to a house. The latter carefully ascertains the requirements and desires of clients. The architect considers available resources: environment, materials, money. He or she draws preliminary sketches, then detailed working drawings. When faced with practical problems, the architect must be willing to depart from the original plan and substitute revisions. Dare we give any less consideration to the design of our homes than the architect gives to a house plan?

An architect designs a foundation to be firm and strong; so a homemaker must design a solid foundation with indestructible building stones: order and routine reinforced with custom and ceremony; memories, values, and beliefs bonded by wisdom and love.

An architect plans walls and roof to ensure protection from the elements; so a homemaker must guard her family from outside threats and internal disintegration by fortifying the sheltering elements: family unity strengthened by shared experience, courtesy, and love; open communication fostered by sensitivity and acceptance; compassionate service beyond the family.

An architect specifies interior partitions and passageways to accommodate diverse functions and relationships and transitions from one activity to another; likewise, a homemaker must create a physical environment that accommodates diverse activities and personalities while preserving the sanctity of the forms and functions that undergird the household: individuality and unity; solitude and sociality; work and leisure.

# PROLOGUE: WHAT IS HOME?

Architectural considerations extend beyond basic structural demands to important functional and decorative details of a house. An architect reveals his or her personal style through these structural details and ornamentation; a homemaker expresses herself through the furnishing and decoration of her home.

An architect designs doors to permit proper access to the house; a homemaker opens these doors to embrace outsiders. An architect provides windows to frame the out-of-doors; a homemaker must develop vistas beyond her home to formulate a comprehensive worldview. Finally, an architect plans the transition to maturity, knowing full well that the very path that leads the children home each day will someday lead them away.

By many, architecture is considered to be the mother of all the arts—*archi* means "master," while *tectu* means "to build." I am in a sense an architect: a master builder. But mine is the building of homes: homemaker. My credo is that of George Herbert: "Study this art; make it thy grand design."

# CHAPTER 1
# FOUNDATIONS:
# "BUILD SURE IN THE BEGINNING"*

*An architect designs a foundation to be firm and strong. Likewise a homemaker must design her solid foundation with indestructible building stones.*

---

*James Russell Lowell

# DEEPER THAN REMEMBRANCE

*These building stones include order
and routine reinforced by custom
and ceremony: memories, values,
and beliefs bonded by wisdom and
love.*

"Mom! Can this room be mine?" Kimberly pleads, pulling me into an empty second-story room overlooking the spacious backyard.

"You won't believe the size of the attic!" David pokes his head from the doorway off a landing leading to the attic steps.

"Be careful you don't bump your head against the eaves," I warn. "Nails are sticking out from the ceiling boards."

Jonathan appears at the top of the hallway stairs, shirt soiled and face covered with dirt. "I was down in the basement. It's *spooky!*"

"Don't go down there," David advises. "It's just meant to house the heater."

"But it's fun. There's this neat place where you can crawl under the house."

"It's so dirty. Look! You've tracked dirt up the stairs," I point out.

"Jonathan, you've got to see the attic," urges David, trying to distract the subterranean explorer. "C'mon, let's check it out."

When Dave returns and the children continue their

# CHAPTER 1

explorations, he and I walk through the empty rooms savoring the character of the big old house with its high ceilings, stained-glass window, quaint nooks and corners. Visualizing our possessions in the newly acquired manse, we place our walnut table in the dining room; we stretch our furniture out across the front room extending the full width of the house. We imagine high-backed rocking chairs and a hanging swing on the wrap-around porch.

Six years have passed since that day. Furnished now with people, memories, and traditions, this boxy structure set on a large corner lot bordered with thick hedges has become for us a symbol of stability, the anchor point of our lives. It is the launching pad from which we embark on our various activities; it is the harbor that protects at night. It is *home*.

Yet even as I acknowledge my attachment to this place, I feel a pang of longing. I yearn for the assurance of permanency. Will this house welcome our children home from college? Will grandchildren delight in its particular joys and comforts? W. B. Yeats poignantly sounded my heart-longings for roots in "A Prayer for My Daughter": "O may she live like some green laurel / Rooted in one dear perpetual place."[1]

Roots are essential to a sense of security. Attachment to something other than ourselves—something solid and stable—provides us with a sense of identity and a continuity throughout the changing stages of our lives.

Some people anchor their roots to a country, perhaps their place of origin. Others sink their roots in a given terrain. Irish poet Patrick Kavanagh mused,

A month ago I was lying on the side of a hill,
    looking at one of the loveliest landscapes in

Ireland. I was just back from a short reading tour in America where I had earned more in a month than a term's teaching at home would bring. But at no point in my journey, even crossing a sunlit campus after my morning's stint was done, or relaxing in some heated pool, was I as happy as that May day, on the slopes of Shiabh Gullion.[2]

For me, uprooted from my place of childhood and youth, our house has become my fixed point. I find myself deliberately setting my roots in our home—the one place I can immediately claim and make my own. Yet even as I sink my roots deeper into this soil I call home, I know we have no certainty that we will always live here. This home is in fact more a symbol than the reality of permanence.

How, then, can I satisfy my longing for roots? How can I provide my family with the identity and security derived from a sense of place when we have not always lived here and may someday feel led to move away? Indeed, upon what does anyone in our mobile society ground his or her security? Reassuring as it may be to anchor one's existence in the permanence of place, it is not an option for many or a guarantee for any.

If we want confidence more dependable than the caprice of circumstance, our foundation must be firmer than any country, culture, or terrain, more durable than the brick and mortar on which our present homes rest. We must build our homes on foundations made with indestructible building stones: order and routines reinforced by custom and ceremony; memories and traditions cemented with repetition; values and beliefs bonded by wisdom and love. We must establish our homes on strong spiritual heritages anchored with roots deeper than remembrance.

29

## CHAPTER 1

The foundation of a building is the essential base, the part on which all other parts rest. I've read building manuals that prescribe precise formulas to determine how deep and thick footings and foundation walls should be. *Funk and Wagnalls Standard Primer* promises, "If these formulas of size and mixture are followed, you will have satisfactory footings, and the house will be started properly in the beginning."[3]

Unlike the undergirding footings and foundation walls of a house, the formulas for the spiritual foundations of a home are not precise. Yet the principle could not be clearer: All rests on an essential base. As James Russell Lowell has written, "Build sure in the beginning."

How comforting it would be to know that our children will be able to return through the years to the shelter and embrace of this lovely home. Yet even the most permanent place on earth is not an adequate foundation. I must let my longings for physical roots serve as a constant reminder: to build our home on an intangible foundation that will stand firm against the storms of time and transition.

### YOUR STORY

1. Which of the houses you have inhabited most represents "home" to you?
2. How do you feel about your present home?
3. Describe your dream house.
4. With your available resources what can you do to make your house or apartment seem more like home?

# DELIGHTFUL MY INHERITANCE
## STONES OF FAMILY HERITAGE

Dancing shadows cast by leafy branches lengthen on the lawn. I linger at the picnic table, savoring my last sip of lemonade. Around me a kaleidoscope of activities unite four generations of Huffmans. I hear the intermittent crack of croquet mallets hitting balls, the rhythmic "ping-pong, ping-pong" of a spirited game of table tennis, the shouts, laughter, and wails of young children who let porch doors slam behind them. Women carry remains of salads and casseroles into the kitchen while the men fold tables and extinguish glowing embers in the barbecue pit.

Almost two decades have passed since returning to the Indiana lake site that, throughout the summers of my childhood, united the families of my father and his two brothers. Since our last gathering a new generation has been born. My older cousins are now grandmothers; then they were mothers of young children.

The most poignant evidence of the passage of time, however, is the silver-haired group seated in porch swings and rockers. My father and mother are deeply engaged in conversation with dad's sister-in-law. I'm sharply reminded of our recent losses: My aunt's husband has passed on.

Absent, also, is the middle brother whose wife of fifty-some years has died.

Suddenly I'm overcome with the powerful mix of emotions that has been building within me since our arrival here at this place laden with so many memories. Desiring to be alone with my past, I walk the road to the canal, where a rowboat is anchored to a concrete retaining wall. Untying the rope, I shove the boat from shore and quickly jump in. After a few wild whacks with the oars, I set my course lakeward, establishing a rhythmic drop-pull-lift, drop-pull-lift.

The frame cottage gets smaller and smaller as I glide toward the center of the lake. Moving people-shapes recede. My attention shifts to the lake shoreline—familiar contours of the ten-acre seminary campus that was my childhood territory.

I rest my oars against the edge of the boat. Diamond-drops of water fall from the paddles to create concentric rings upon the lake's surface. Colors reflecting the low sun set the shimmering waters afire. In the distance a familiar roar announces cars racing at the county fairground. The scent of the lake water, the sight of a bird skimming its surface, and the evening sounds of crickets, frogs, and motorboats transform me into that child of thirty summers past, reluctant to see the sun disappear below the horizon, the signal of bedtime.

Surveying the panorama of seminary buildings, I am flooded by waves of memories. Looming in the foreground is the wood-framed residential building—our summer habitat and the base of my operation. From its large picture window I would observe flash storms, the rain advancing like a mighty regiment across dark waters. The sprawling patio was the center of countless activities: maneuvering the families of dolls who lived on its satellites to each side; reading while awaiting the magical hour of 3:00 P.M. when the lifeguard would assume duty; sipping mint-sprigged lemonade while relaxing on lawn chairs; watching the setting of the sun with my family.

A nearby cluster of faculty cottages evoke a memory of the exhilarating approach of a new school term that would bring new families. My gaze follows the gravel path past the administration building and the outdoor amphitheater—site of countless cookouts and programs, sermons and sing-alongs—to the dining hall, the communal center.

I study the natural landmarks that have defined hours upon hours of play: the weeping willow in which I kept a sentinel watch, secretly observing passersby below; clumps of berry bushes from which I shaped the rooms and corridors of an entire community of playhouses; the sandy beach where I dug castles and modeled dozens of cookies and cupcakes for my "bakery shop." How many times a day did I run the full length of the campus on the precarious irregular sea-wall, stopping occasionally to scoop up a small frog or a handful of forget-me-nots? Even now, after three decades, I can feel that euphoric sense of independence that was mine for three magical months when Dad, preoccupied with school business, and Mother, lulled by an elastic summer schedule and safe community, set me free, save for the most elemental boundaries of mealtimes, naptimes, and bedtimes.

At this moment the brother and parents, the aunts, uncles, and cousins of my past seem more immediate than the strangers assembled at the nearby lake home. Watching the fireflies light the darkening skies with tiny flickering torches, it would hardly surprise me to see Grandfather Huffman, the patriarch of his irrepressible sons, strolling across the campus, towel hanging over his arm, ready for his evening swim.

A wave of nostalgia washes over me. I'm lonesome for people and places past. I'm lonesome for the child that was I—cared for, protected, oblivious to the concerns and responsibilities of those who provided such security. Today's time lapse triggers a sudden flash of recognition: This place in panorama before me represents the single cord that unifies all the significant landscapes of my life. During each June of my first ten summers, my family made an annual pilgrimage from New England to this lakeside campus where my father assumed administrative responsibilities for the summer program of Winona Lake School of Theology. In my tenth year when we made a major move west, it became the firm ground upon which I stayed my heart until I could be firmly established in the foreign soil of Illinois. Even after my marriage I returned in the summer with my ministry-bound husband. During his years of youth work in Michigan, we returned with carloads of young people to attend retreat weekends.

Now we return again, this time with our children, to establish the connecting link between this place and our Florida abode of more than a decade. This time I see the haunts of my early years through the eyes of David, Kimberly, and Jonathan.

What do my children see in this place? What do I want them to see? I want to introduce them to my past, I suppose: places and people meaningful to me. Yet even more than physical realities, I want them to recognize certain values engendered for me by this place: carefree summer days, a freedom to roam, an acquaintance with special people, the security of extended family. In a real sense I want them to experience what I had—this rich heritage that marked my early summers and informed my years beyond.

Even as I define certain longings quickened by my nostalgic return, I know I can't reproduce my past for my children any more than I can return to it myself. Indeed their experience, like mine, is unique, and yet my experience does determine part of their heritage. The past is always with us, informing and defining our present.

Of course, their father also contributes to this distinct heritage. Together our lives provide a rich blend of two separate heritages—a merger of values and beliefs, traditions and customs.

At home on our bedroom wall is a collage of photographs—a visual representation of this intangible reality: the white-frame Norwegian church in which Dave's paternal great-grandmother was christened and married; his missionary parents posed in formal wedding attire in a Chinese courtyard; the weathered Michigan farmhouse of my maternal grandparents; the white Cape-Cod-style home of my parents. Snapshots and memorabilia from our separate childhoods are interspersed among the pictorial archives of our ancestors. The focal point of this mix is our engraved wedding invitation announcing the imminent union between these two families. The photographs of our children reveal the unique synthesis of this genetic blend.

No, I can't go backward in time. I can't reproduce the details of my past for my children. I shouldn't even want to. Our spiritual and physical legacy to them—conscious or unconscious, good or bad—forms a part of their lives as much as hidden foundation blocks form a part of the house set upon them. Our challenge is to construct for our children a broad and firm foundation by sifting through our separate

pasts and selecting where we can. Then, perhaps, someday
they can say with the psalmist:

Lord, you have assigned me my portion and my cup;
    you have made my lot secure.
The boundary lines have fallen for me in pleasant
        places;
    surely, I have a delightful inheritance. (Ps. 16:5–6)

## YOUR STORY

1. What aspects of your childhood hold the deepest
   meaning for you?
2. What people and places have had the greatest influence
   on your life?
3. What elements from your background and your
   spouse's background would you like to transmit to
   your children?
4. What unique contribution have you made to your
   children's legacy?
5. If you could write a "spiritual will" for your children,
   what would you include?

# PLACES OF THE HEART
# STONES OF LOCATION

"There's Bok Tower! I'm the first to see Bok Tower!" sings a voice from the back seat of the car. I feel a catch of anticipation as I sight the familiar landmark etched against a stained-glass sky splotched with rain clouds. To this subtropical landscape we're returning after our long vacation north: Glossy-green citrus groves roll east of the highway toward the distant tower; to the west, palmetto scrub hugs the flat terrain, dotted intermittently with tall long-leaf pines and isolated clumps of cabbage palms.

As we travel the remaining miles separating us from our present home, I can't help but recall my response to this same land when we first arrived in Florida. Out the car window I then stared at the sandy terrain, longing for summer meadows of cornflowers, black-eyed Susan, and Queen Anne's lace. Gazing at stiltlike pines capped with contorted limbs fringed with tufts of long needles, I ached for dense, green woodlands. I scarcely noticed the pride-of-the-ridge citrus groves, my attention riveted on billboards boasting sun-land attractions. When, at last, I opened the car door at our destination, my heart was as heavy as the hot and humid air.

Even as I gradually adjusted to new circumstances and

developed new friendships, I continued to struggle with a genuine sense of alienation from the land. I felt radically severed from the reassuring cycle of seasons and all that it spoke to me of beauty and renewal. I remained homesick for things I had previously taken as for granted as the rising and setting of the sun: the brilliant turn of autumn color; the whitewash of snow; the procession of spring bulb-flowers heralded by the first crocus; soft blades of summer grass between bare toes.

In an all-out effort to combat these feelings, I sought places reminiscent of my roots and claimed them for my own. I strived to create a home atmosphere evocative of places past: silk spring flowers in containers throughout the house; a blue and white kitchen—a faithful reproduction of the one I had left behind in our Dutch-influenced Michigan community. I compensated for the lack of vivid seasonal changes by concentrating on traditions surrounding the cyclical holy days and holidays.

As important as my efforts were to settle into our new location, they were not enough. Total adjustment required a "moment of truth" resulting from two unrelated incidents.

The first transpired at the home of a friend. When I commented on a newly acquired painting, my friend said it was a gift from her husband, fulfilling her desire to own a painting by the talented regional artist Robert Butler. The work depicted a Florida dear to her heart, she explained, the place of her childhood.

I studied the framed scene. It was a familiar Florida landscape: a stream meandering through marsh scrubland, a bay-head with a cluster of trees—tall Florida pine flanked by cabbage palms, a cypress, and maybe an oak. Several ducks dotted the sky. A forest of pines lined the horizon. The painting portrayed the very Florida I had rejected. Yet as I

viewed this landscape, I began to see it through new eyes—
her eyes: the eyes of love.

Soon after this exchange, I was given a copy of
Marjorie Kinnan Rawlings's *Cross Creek*. Three pages into
the book, I stopped short at these words: "No other place
seems possible to us, just as when truly in love none other
offers the comfort of the beloved."[4] The "place" of which
she spoke was her native central Florida, the place depicted
in my friend's painting.

I continued reading, now with the posture of a student,
permitting the author's loving descriptions to instruct me in
the wonders of this subtropical region. She guided me
through the gentle cycle of seasons, teaching me the subtle
gradations of flora and fauna, introducing me to the habits
and habitats of bird and beast. A love story, *Cross Creek*: the
smitten describing the beguiling ways of her beloved.

I could not remain indifferent. I made my discovery:
My very efforts to stake claim to this place had been, in fact,
a rejection of that which was unique to it. I had sought and
claimed those things reminiscent of a northern clime. As
helpful as that had been to my initial adjustment, it was an
inadequate basis for a complete adjustment. My appreciation
of Florida was limited to those things that met my standard
of beauty. Implicit in that standard was a rejection of that
which was indigenous to this land, denying its unique
character as well as limiting my enjoyment.

With *Cross Creek* as my textbook and Miss Rawlings as
my teacher, I started to see a new Florida: the majestic
perfection of the magnolia tree; life within the moss
festooning the oak trees; redbirds darting among palms
entwined with trumpet vines. I began to anticipate and thrill
to subtle seasonal changes: the breaking of summer into
fresh autumn; colorful winter offerings—pink and white

# CHAPTER 1

camellia blooms, shiny, red holly berries, citrus trees bearing luminous globes of orange and yellow; spring air scented with orange blossom, azalea bushes bedecked in pastel finery; the mad exuberance of summer growth, flash storms dumping welcome relief from heat and humidity.

The lesson I learned was to accept a place for what it is, to surrender myself to its particular cadence and rhythm. "If you would learn the song of the land," mused Robert Blanding in *Floridays,* "you must look and listen and . . . understand. You must root your heart in tropic soil."[5] C. S. Lewis advocated a "serious, yet gleeful determination to rub one's nose in the very quiddity of each thing—to rejoice in its being (so magnificently) what it is."[6]

I don't know if I'll ever respond to an acre of palmetto as I do to a meadow of wildflowers. Rawlings herself acknowledged: "Along with our deep knowledge of the earth is a preference of each of us for certain kinds of it, for the earth is as various as we are various."[7] But I have come to appreciate central Florida for its singular offerings without comparing it to any other place.

Those other dear places will always remain close to me in a secret region in my heart to which I can return when my spirit needs nourishment from the past. As Anne Morrow Lindbergh wrote, they will "always be a part of the permanent landscape of the mind and that is enough."[8] Indeed, many such places are represented throughout our present home. A childhood of memories is contained on our living-room mantel in a spray of silk dogwood in a cranberry glass flask. On the "Key Biscayne shelf" in the morning room, ten summers of beach vacation are collected in assorted memorabilia.

Above the writing desk in the morning room hangs a treasured gift—our own Robert Butler painting of moss-draped oaks bending toward a creek reflecting cameo clouds on Wedgwood blue skies. Whenever I view this landscape, I'm reminded to be receptive to the unique possibilities of this place, of *every* place. Each place—past, present, and future—makes its own special contribution to the ever-broadening landscapes of the mind: those pleasant places of the heart.

## YOUR STORY

1. What geographical terrain is dearest to your heart?
2. What are the limitations of your present locale? What are its strengths?
3. In what ways can you take greater advantage of the natural and cultural resources of your local area?

# THE BEAUTY OF THE HOUSE
# STONES OF ORDER AND ROUTINE

The children are in school and Dave is at the office. I pour myself a mug of coffee, put some Mozart on the stereo, and retreat to our morning room to enjoy a few moments of solitude. How pleasant to be settled into the rhythm and routine of our autumn schedule. Summer offers special joys with its elastic hours, but I welcome September and a more productive, ordered life. Dave and I have conferred with each child concerning his or her activities—clubs, sports, music lessons, and practice schedules. We have negotiated over bedtimes, allowances, study hours. As a family we have attempted to integrate our diverse schedules, hammering out compromises when necessary. With the finished schedule written in ink on the official calendar, we have resumed our full back-to-school stride!

As satisfactory as that completed schedule seems, I know my task has only begun. It is one thing to coordinate activities of five people, each going in a different direction, but something more challenging to maintain such a schedule. However perfect it might appear on paper, it is always subject to change, torpedoed by interruptions. And then its success ultimately depends on effective enforcement. It is not enough to plan events and responsibilities on a calendar; the plan must be implemented. I know full well, even as I relish these elusive moments of ordered serenity, that the task of keeping the family ordered will fall on me: chauffeur, musical coach, cook, laundry sorter, clock watcher, homework supervisor.

In the intriguing book *She: Understanding Feminine Psychology,* Robert Johnson considered the relationship between a woman's tasks and her development as a person. He examined the myth of Amor and Psyche for insights into a woman's evolution into full feminine consciousness. The ancient story begins with a king and queen who have three daughters. Psyche, the youngest, is so beautiful that she is worshiped by the people. This inevitably enrages Aphrodite—the goddess of femininity—who decrees the judgment that Psyche is to marry Death. Aphrodite instructs her son Eros—the god of love—to enflame Psyche with love for the loathsome beast Death, who will claim her and thus end Psyche's challenge to Aphrodite.

As fate would have it, Eros accidentally pricks his finger on one of his arrows, falls in love with Psyche himself, and takes her as his bride on condition that she will not look at him or inquire into any of his ways. All is paradise until one night, when, at the prodding of her jealous sisters, Psyche brings a lamp to view her sleeping husband. For her disobedience Psyche is doomed. She's given only one hope for deliverance: by performing four nearly impossible tasks prescribed by Aphrodite.

The first of these four famous tasks (which represent the four stages in Psyche's inner development toward wholeness as a woman) is to sort a huge pile of seeds into separate piles before nightfall. Robert Johnson sees in this task a beautiful symbol: "In many of the practical matters of life, in the running of a household, for example, a woman's task is to see that form, or order, prevails. That is sorting.

What household has not echoed to the cry of 'Mom, where is my other sock?' "9 Recognizing modern woman's resistance to this particular task, Johnson maintains the "act of sorting" is not only necessary for order in the family, but is "a primary requirement for her development."

(Some might argue about gender: Is "seed sorting" really the woman's role? Johnson envisions a movement toward wholeness for both men and women, the complete Janus-faced personality, each person facing simultaneously inner and outer worlds that have traditionally been gender stereotyped.)

In our home, however (for practical reasons), I am the logical one to assume "seed sorting" tasks. *I'm here.* I'm the first to sense the absence of order, and I'm the first to suffer the consequences. In the process of "sifting and sorting," I discover I am truly nourished. Something good happens to me as I assume the task of seed sorting. When I "see that form, or order, prevails" in the household, my spirit fills with peace.

"The beauty of the house is order" reads a sampler in cross-stitch given to me some twenty years ago at a wedding shower. Along with the remaining sips of my coffee I savor the beauty of rare ordered moments, knowing the end may be only a ringing phone or doorbell away. Likewise, I realize my tranquil morning-room moments, infrequent as they are, constitute only one of the many rewards of a well-ordered life!

> First Peace and Silence all disputes control,
>     Then Order plays the soul;
> And giving all things their set form and hours,
>     Makes of wild wood sweet walks and bowers.
>                                         —George Herbert

## YOUR STORY

1. What factors within your family habitually rule against an ordered life?
2. Who in your household assumes the greatest responsibility for coordinating individual schedules?
3. List the activities of each family member. In what ways can you strengthen or streamline the family schedule to establish a more ordered household?

# AGREEABLE HOURS
# STONES OF CUSTOM AND CEREMONY

*There are few hours in life more*
*agreeable than the hour dedicated*
*to the ceremony known as afternoon*
*tea.*

—*Henry James*

"Mom? When are we going to start having high tea again?" queries Jonathan.

I look at my denim-clad inquirer with amusement and delight. Standing before me wearing a Boston Red Sox cap atop tousled hair, he looks an unlikely candidate for such a refinement. Yet I'm enormously pleased that he wishes to reinstitute the Sunday afternoon ritual we have observed most of his lifetime, though not during this past summer. Our rendition of this time-honored observance would doubtless raise the eyebrows of our English forebears, still, when the tea trolley bearing peanut butter and jelly "tea sandwiches," fruit, cake, and punch is wheeled into the living room, they would have to give a slight nod of approval. And surely such ceremony suppresses the laughter of the occasional young cynical guest who questions the necessity of our weekly, family read-aloud sessions.

There are many aspects of teatime that appeal to me— arranging our prettiest china, silver, and linen napkins, or savoring at leisure both goodies and good company. But I suspect my zeal for tea parties was implanted at an early age by my tea-loving mother, who presided over the tea tray at the dinner table. With mounting anticipation we children waited for her to pour tea into the last porcelain cup. Then she would slice a rich dessert elegantly displayed on its pedestal dish. Or she would set a silver tray of dainty sandwiches and cookies beside the lusterware tea service on the table in front of the sofa.

The ceremony of afternoon teatime was made fashionable in the eighteenth century by the Duchess of Bedford, who experienced a "sinking feeling" each afternoon around four. Once established, teatime became an instant hit, first in England and Russia and eventually in America. This delightful habit of afternoon tea is enjoying a revival in America, as a growing number of hotels and restaurants are now offering this welcome respite to weary travelers or shoppers.

What could be behind this current resurgence of this dated institution? Certain words recur in discussions of the custom: rite, ritual, tradition, ceremony, occasion. In its present form, a common element of afternoon tea is a relaxed communion between host and guest, based on the aesthetic etiquette of serving tea. Could our fast-food, push-button society need this time-honored tradition to offset the threat of chaos? The rudimentary elements of survival go beyond function—drinking and eating—to the celebration of life, beauty, and friendship.

In his introduction to Milton's *Paradise Lost*, C. S. Lewis referred to the "proper pleasure of ritual." Lewis continued: "The ceremony provides the form, the ritual which renders pleasures less fugitive . . . which hands over to the power of wise custom the task (to which the individual and his moods are so inadequate) of being festive or sober, gay or reverent, when we choose to be, and not at the bidding of chance."[10]

Teatime, in essence, takes a common activity and makes it uncommon by means of ceremony and custom.

Ceremony of any kind elevates the ordinary above mere function. Through ceremony—a prescribed ritual of performance—we dignify the commonplace; through custom—the repetition of that ritual—we remind ourselves again and again of its higher meaning. Simply stated: All is uncommon *if we make it so.*

Everyday routines such as drinking tea can be dignified and elevated through ceremony and custom. Meals, for example: One can serve and eat food on the run—or even substitute a pill—and fulfill the necessity of consumption. Or one could sit before a beautifully laden table, experience a variety of foods served in successive courses, relish conversation with fellow diners—and transcend a common function with accoutrements of beauty and friendship. Thomas Howard has said, "If this commonplace of daily life bears this sort of freight, then we do well to deck it. Candles for birthdays, bouquets for weddings, parchment for graduations—and the table set for breakfast."[11]

Alexandra Stoddard, in *Living a Beautiful Life,* has observed a tendency to save up a sense of the special for a few outstanding events each year—for a particular party, anniversary, or birthday celebration, a vacation.

Such events comprise, at the most, five percent of our living time, and the remaining ninety-five percent is often merely walked through in wistful anticipation of some later joy. But what we all really want to do, I think, is *live* in the present, really enjoy every day, not put our lives on hold for that special five percent. . . . Special events should be exclamation marks in our lives, but ordinary days need to be celebrations too, as meaningful and beautiful as the big events.[12]

# AGREEABLE HOURS

The ordinary functions, when bedecked and festooned with ceremony, become occasions—from awakening in the morning, through the events of the workday, to the bedtime rituals at night. Each activity of our lives is an opportunity for celebration and ceremony, creativity and pleasure. Each task can be dignified by the beauty of ritual and hallowed by the larger truth it represents. As we weave the warp of ceremony and custom through the woof of routine and duty, we reinforce and strengthen the fabric of our daily existence.

Afternoon tea with all its customs and rituals provides a gentle means to elevate function. May we learn a lesson from its timeless appeal to turn the countless common actions of life into uncommon ones through custom and ceremony!

## YOUR STORY

1. Do you remember with delight particular customs or rituals from your childhood? List several.
2. What customs or rituals add interest to the fabric of your family's routine living?
3. Consider your schedule. In what ways can you enrich the following routines for yourself and for your family: mealtimes, household chores, return from work or school, evening study hours, bedtime?
4. What events and transitions can you highlight through family celebrations (such as, end of a school/work week; new week, month, or season; birthdays)?

# GARRET GALLERY
## STONES OF MEMORIES

We awaken to a cool, breezy day—the first break in the autumn's relentless heat. I decide to devote the day to a long-delayed task: cleaning the attic. The weather for it is perfect, neither too hot nor cold.

I climb the steep stairs to the musty garret. Light from three dormers reveals the magnitude of my chore: Boxes are stacked in disarray in the crawl space to the left of the stair; toys, tables, and a clutter of books, magazines, and papers cover the large central area. To my right, paper bags, boxes, and clothing are strewn about under the sloping eaves.

Where to begin? I decide to tackle the clothing first. Reaching into the closest mound I pick out items randomly one at a time, forming separate piles: save; discard; Goodwill. I salvage an occasional toy buried in the cloth; I discover a wooden angel long missing from its Swiss music box. I set aside the diaper bag filled with Kimberly's baby clothes. (Will she ever again dress Susie in these clothes, or should I give them away?) Nearby I spot a diaphanous heap of pink and yellow chiffon: my party dresses from high school. Returning them to the "dress-up suitcase," I can't help but realize how close Kimberly now is to this make-believe world of high-heels, formals, and jewelry. Finished,

I proudly survey distinct mountains of clothing that have replaced the original chaotic heaps.

Next I begin sorting through a disarray of books, magazines, and paper that clutters the central portion. Beside an old wooden school desk is a file case from my teaching days. Beyond I spy rulers, pencils, scissors, and worksheets on makeshift tables—props for the children's game of "school."

On to "Craig Corner." Here are remnants from the library of our home's former occupant, an elderly single woman who bequeathed her home to our church to be used as its manse. Shelf after shelf of books reveal the wide-ranging interests of this remarkable woman who undertook an African safari in her youth and whose exotic plants were featured in horticultural magazines. I scan the spines of the varied volumes. Recurring subjects reveal her diverse interests: renaissance history, murder mysteries, travel books, self-improvement guides, literary sourcebooks, fiction. On the top shelf I spot a *Tourist Guide to Mexico*. An article about Mexico is folded into its pages along with a slip of paper noting the value of the peso. Did she take that trip to Mexico? Paging through several other books with underlinings, marginal notes, inserted gray monogrammed stationery, news clippings, letters, and postcards (all give whimsical insight into their unusual owner), I resist a temptation to linger, promising myself a return visit on another day!

On to the array of luggage—mostly battered relics of my childhood. Side by side I align my blue Skyway suitcases, an accumulation of several season's worth of Christmas and birthday gifts. Countless memories are packed in their ample interiors, for they accompanied me to slumber parties, on high school choir tours, a graduation trip

# CHAPTER 1

to Europe, and our honeymoon. Now our children pack these bags for their overnights and summer vacation trips!

Memories surge over me as I shift boxes filled with more than twenty years' accumulation of Christmas decorations: ornaments, wreaths, candles, pillows, evergreen ropes, and a box marked "fragile" containing our precious olive-wood crèche. I start to anticipate the Advent season, rich in festivity and tradition.

One box buried deep in a corner catches my attention. Pulling it into the light, I lift its lid and reach into yellowed tissue. I remove layer after layer of crisp paper until I discover at the bottom—Beth, my favorite doll, her plaster face lined with age. My entire childhood of playing with dolls lies within this cardboard box!

Rearranging several large boxes filled with cast-off curtains and bedspreads, I pull a rectangular box into the light. Opening its lid, I uncover my complete collection of journals, scrapbooks, and memorabilia from high school and college. I chuckle aloud at the memory of their near-disastrous fate. When we moved to Lake Wales, we placed several boxes in a storage room at church. The room, unbeknown to us, housed a vast assortment of articles destined for the annual men-of-the-church rummage sale. On the day of the sale, a puzzled deacon knocked at Dave's office door and queried, "Are you sure you want to auction off this box?"—this very box filled with the complete documentation of our youth!

Digging under diplomas and athletic letters, I come to a packet of cards and letters from our high school romance. Dave's sophomore class photo stares up at me—his eyes younger than his own namesake's. I finger through the letters, from our first summer's separation, featuring light-hearted accounts of high school trivia, on to those exchanged during the engagement summer—plans for a wedding and shared life. A packet of programs, notes, and cards reveals a parenthesis in our relationship: our first year of college during which we agreed to separate so we could "get to know others."

Memories . . . truly this attic is a gallery of memories! Boxed, shelved, and stored under the four eaves are sculptures, art objects, books, and manuscripts documenting the ages and stages of our family's existence. Each relic— rare or commonplace—evokes scores of pictures etched by memory's camera.

Today's task was made more pleasurable by this stroll through my Garret Gallery. Yet memories have greater significance than simple sentiment. Memories permit our past to continue into the present, providing us with an important sense of continuity. "Long did I build you, oh house!" wrote Louis Guilliame in *Les Lettres*. "With each memory I carried stones from the bank to your topmost wall."[13] Yes, an entire past may dwell in our present places if we consciously (or unconsciously) build our houses with stones from the past. As the saying goes, "We bring our lares and penates with us." We furnish our homes with our history and our heritage.

We gain a sense of perspective as we view our present in the light of our past: Recalling how we survived those difficult moments—wet, colicky babies or demanding toddlers—provides us encouragement for the stresses of later childhood and adolescence. Even bad memories can provide valuable reminders of tough lessons and their eventual redemption.

Sometimes, during darkest days, memories are all we have. Dietrich Bonhoeffer's *Letters and Papers from Prison* gives repeated poignant testimony to the beneficial work of

memories during difficult days. In his Christmas letter to his
parents in 1943, he wrote,

> But for years you have given us such perfectly
> lovely Christmases that our grateful recollection of
> them is strong enough to put a darker one into the
> background. It's not till such times as these that
> we realize what it means to possess a past and a
> spiritual inheritance independent of changes of
> time and circumstance. The consciousness of
> being borne up by a spiritual tradition that goes
> back for centuries gives one a feeling of confidence
> and security in the face of all passing strains and
> stresses. I believe that anyone who is aware of
> such reserves of strength needn't be ashamed of
> more tender feelings evoked by the memory of a
> rich and noble past, for in my opinion they belong
> to the better and nobler part of mankind. They
> will not overwhelm those who hold fast to values
> that no one can take from them.[14]

Later, on the occasion of his father's birthday, Bonhoeffer recalled the memories of the previous years and
warned, "We oughtn't to allow ourselves to be deprived of
the inner possession of a splendid past by a temporarily
troubled present."[15]

Not only are memories a help during present trouble
but they suggest the hope of a better future. On his own
birthday Bonhoeffer wrote to a close friend, recalling
memories of eight successive birthdays they had celebrated
together: "All those things are delightful recollections that
are proof against the horrible atmosphere of this place."[16]

The special shared experiences of today are an investment in my children's Gallery of Memories. Who knows what memory might provide a light in a future dark place . . . a noble reminder of what a good time can really be . . . a hope for a better tomorrow.

The word *garret* is derived from an old French term *garite,* meaning "place of refuge." Dostoyevski, through the character of Alyosha, in *The Brothers Karamazov* declared,

> My dear children . . . You must know that there is nothing higher and stronger and more wholesome and useful for life in after years than some good memory, especially a memory connected with childhood, with home. People talk to you a great deal about your education, but some fine, sacred memory, preserved from childhood, is perhaps the best education. If a man carries many such memories with him into life, he is safe to the end of his day, and if we have only one good memory left in our hearts, even that may sometime be the means of saving us.

Memories. They are always with us, increasing in value yet requiring neither a safe deposit box nor insurance. Paradoxically, from memories stored in the "garret galleries" of our minds, we fortify the foundations of our home— for ourselves and for our children.

> Tis hope, and joy, and memory give
> A home in which the heart can live.
>
> Anonymous

## YOUR STORY

1. List several of your happiest childhood and adult memories. What made them so special?

# CHAPTER 1

2. Not all memories are good ones. In what ways can the bad experiences be used for good in your life?
3. Today plan some activity that will be an investment in your family's Gallery of Memories.
4. Purchase a blank notebook in which you can record special family events and store photography and memorabilia. Set aside time occasionally to share the contents of this memory book with each child.

# THE CORNERSTONE OF TRUTH
## STONES OF VALUES AND BELIEFS

"We were supposed to write about a life experience that taught us an important lesson," Kimberly explains, handing me an essay titled "Wrong Way."

I read her essay, which recalls an incident from years past. She had been granted permission to walk home alone from school, provided she came "directly home." How clearly I can visualize Kimberly's arrival, a full forty-five minutes later than my most generous time allowance. How heated was her protest: "I did come straight home. Honest, I did." I continued to plead for truthfulness; she insisted that her improbable version was true.

The conflict was resolved that evening when Dave returned from work. "Kimberly, I talked to Mr. Diaz today. He said he saw you in his neighborhood."

Kimberly's face was a study in guilt as her father inadvertently revealed the incriminating evidence that she had indeed been at the far side of the lake where her buddy Michelle lived.

Now, two years later, Kimberly extols truthfulness by expanding her experience of walking the "wrong way" to *living* the wrong way. C. S. Lewis universalized the effectiveness of lessons from experience in his autobiography *Surprised by Joy*.

> What I like about experience is that it is such an honest thing. You may take any number of wrong turnings; but keep your eyes open and you'll not be allowed to go very far before the warning signs appear. You may have deceived yourself, but experience is not trying to deceive you. The universe rings true whenever you fairly test it.[17]

Kimberly's excursion into lying contains in microcosm elements common to all detours from truth. It began with good intentions. But the sunny day, her classmate, time to spare, and a heady sense of independence worked together toward the erroneous rationalization: "It's not so much longer the other way home. If I hurry, I can walk with Michelle and still be home in time. No one need ever know."

Confronted with reality ("Where did the time go?"), she found it infinitely easier to gamble with a lie than face the certain consequences of admitting the truth. In her efforts to convince me, she may have begun to believe herself. Fortunately, her digression from the truth was cut short by the painful experience of an unexpected encounter with the facts.

In the lengthy discussion that ensued, her father and I attempted to explain to her the importance we placed on truth. There was good reason for our directive to come straight home. Although she might disagree, she was expected to obey us. But as alarming as her disobedience was to us, her lie to cover her action was more so.

Why do we place such importance on truthfulness?

Why was Kimberly's punishment for lying much more severe than that for disobedience alone? The spectacle of this woeful creature with puffy eyes and tear-stained cheeks might have moved us to break down and give her another chance. Was her deceptive alibi really so bad?

If we can't elicit trust concerning all of our acts, how can we achieve it in any of them? Misguided or wrong though our deeds may be, if we do not acknowledge the truth about them, we lie to ourselves and cut off honest, open relationships. Ultimately we deny ourselves opportunities for correction and subsequent growth. This incident taught Kimberly a healthy respect for truth. Our hope is that life's continued experience will instill in her a deep *love* for all truth.

"The cornerstone in Truth is laid," wrote hymn writer John Oxenham. Many other stones of virtues complete the foundation on which we establish our homes. Indeed, in *Straight Talk to Men and Their Wives*,[18] child psychologist James Dobson urges parents to instruct their children daily in the following fundamental values: devotion to God, love for humankind, respect for authority, obedience to divine command, self-discipline and self-control, and humbleness of spirit. Each building block is essential in a strong supportive system. But if those virtues are to be strong enough to resist the changing tide of public opinion, the shifting sands of current philosophies, or the racking winds of life's storms, they must be anchored by the cornerstone of truth. Without that cornerstone the house will fall.

The foundation of our home includes many stones: values and beliefs on which we form attitudes and behavior; memories and traditions through which our past informs our present; routines and customs by which we order our days. Love provides the mortar to fill the gaps between stones. No matter how solid the superstructure may be, how efficient the floor plan, how beautiful the decor, if the foundation is not stable, the house will succumb to the storm. One cannot plan too carefully. Build sure . . . build sure in the beginning!

## YOUR STORY

1. Consider your value system. What matters most to you? What do your children and spouse perceive as important to you?
2. On what foundational beliefs of faith do you base your values?
3. In what ways are you strengthening the foundation of your home by instilling the following values:
   devotion to God?
   love for humankind?
   respect for authority?
   obedience to divine command?
   self-discipline and self-control?
   humbleness of spirit?
4. In what respect is love the mortar that holds together the foundational stones of the home?
5. Why is truth the anchoring cornerstone of the house?

# CHAPTER 2
# ROOF AND EXTERIOR WALLS:
# SHELTERING ELEMENTS

*An architect plans walls and roof to ensure protection from adverse weather. Likewise a homemaker must guard her family from outside threats and internal disintegration by fortifying the sheltering elements.*

# A SHELTER IN THE TIME OF STORM

*The sheltering elements include family unity strengthened by shared experience, courtesy, and love; open communication fostered by sensitivity and acceptance; giving beyond the family through compassion and service.*

The sky is a dark, cloudless gray. The ominous quiet is broken by a crash of thunder. Great gusts of wind begin to stir the stillness; assaulted trees bend and sway. Suddenly the sky opens up, releasing its burden of moisture.

Jonathan and I observe the drama outside from our morning-room refuge.

"I love it when it storms," muses Jonathan.

"Why?"

"Because it's so cozy inside."

Feeling snug and secure like a watertight craft adrift the stormy sea, I look around the room glowing with lamplight. Jonathan is nestled deep into the oversized chair, safe from the storm raging outside the glass just inches from his perch.

Nothing emphasizes and tests the protective quality of a house quite so emphatically as hostile elements. Night, rain, snow, howling wind, or wolves contrast the sheltering aspects of a house.

Shelter. The universal appeal of home, whether hut or mansion, centers on the protective, embracing attributes of shelter: light in darkness, dryness in storm, warmth in winter, refuge from wild beasts. Safe and secure is our cozy nest while the elemental forces rage outside. The roof provides a sheltering hood; thick exterior walls wrap a protective shield around interior spaces.

Just as the house serves as a physical shelter from the changing circumstances of nature, the home provides a psychic shelter during the stresses and storms. "This is the true nature of our home," wrote John Ruskin. "It is the place of peace, the shelter not only from all injury but from all terror, doubt, and division." The walls and roof of a house not only provide protection; they signify boundaries that define our personal space. They establish a sense of identity by enclosing our particular collection of people into one perceptible unit.

Social critic Michael Novak has cited the family as society's number one shelter: "Through all the injustices and disasters of the last thousand years, one unforgettable law has been learned: if things go well with family, life is worth living, when the family falters, life falls apart."[1] *Night,* Elie Wiesel's first-person account of life in a Nazi concentration camp, gives strong testimony to the role of the family. Separated forever from his mother and sister, this fifteen-year-old boy's single aim was never to lose sight of his father. Referring to one point when he mistook his father for dead, he wrote: "My mind was invaded suddenly by this realization—there was no more reason to live, no more reason to struggle."[2]

Agree as we may in theory or sentiment about its importance, the family today is, in reality, out of favor. Threatened by busy, divergent lifestyles, isolated geographically from the extended family, weakened by a philosophical ambivalence toward sacrifice and commitment, the family is under unprecedented attack. If we do not actively combat these hostile trends by consciously cultivating family unity, we will encourage its disintegration by default.

## A SHELTER IN THE TIME OF STORM

It is not enough to value family living. We must deliberately strategize for family unity. Just as an architect designs walls and roof to ensure protection from the elements, so parents must consciously build their family unit as a shelter from outside threats and as security from disintegration within. We must develop a strong interlocking network of loyalty by building individual ties to the whole unit as well as to separate members. We must establish and enforce an equitable system of justice so that home is an emotional "safe place" for each person. We must encourage open communication, permitting honest expression of feelings and opinions as well as providing understanding response. We must allocate time to be together—from commonplace daily transactions to the most festive celebrations. Bound together as a strong unified entity, we must reach out in love and service to those beyond the protective boundaries of home.

Frank Lloyd Wright maintained that "organic architecture sees shelter not only as a quality of space but of spirit."[3] Let us likewise view the walls and roof of our shelters not only as protection from exterior forces—human or elemental—but as boundaries of caring that imbue our space with a spirit of love.

## YOUR STORY

1. What place represents safety to you? Why?
2. What factors outside the home pose the greatest threat to the unity of your family?
3. What factors within the home pose the greatest threat to your family's unity?
4. What specific strategies can you employ to strengthen the bond of family?

5. Many families are assaulted by divorce or death. What
   can you do to compensate for such loss within your
   home or to encourage other families that have suffered
   such loss?

# THE BOND OF FAMILY
## SHELTERING ELEMENTS OF
## FAMILY UNITY

"Mom, I'm finished with my homework and there's no special game on television this afternoon. Could I go up to the 'Y' after lunch?" David's hopeful appeal resounds in my ears.

"You know our policy for Sunday afternoons."

"But we don't have any special family plans. It's not as if we have company. There's no conflict with anything else, so why can't I go shoot some baskets for a couple of hours?"

"We've been through this before, David. You know our policy. And I really don't like your putting me in this position."

"Well, I don't understand why I have to stay home when there's a good activity I want to go to—and there's nothing to do at home. What's the difference between playing baseball with the youth group at 4:30 and playing basketball with my friends at 2:30?"

"You know it has nothing to do with the *activity*. It has to do with the particular block of time. All week long each of us is going in a dozen different directions: Dad and I feel we all need a few hours each week when we simply stay home as a family. Sunday afternoon happens to be the only possible time for us."

CHAPTER 2

"But Mom," he pleads, "we're not *doing* anything this afternoon; I always go along with family plans, but it doesn't make sense to stay home to do *nothing*."

"Honey, your father and I reserve a couple of hours Sunday afternoon for all of us to unwind. We've explained this many times. We try to be reasonable if something special comes up, but I don't consider basketball in that category. Don't keep pressing me!"

"I didn't think you'd let me go!" he retorts, turning on his heel and leaving the room.

As I prepare lunch, I mull this confrontation over in my mind. Are we being unreasonable? Should we let him go? We *don't* have any special plans. Basketball certainly is a wholesome activity. David's a good kid. I should be thankful it's basketball and not something bad. Could we lose his support by enforcing this policy too strictly?

Dave and I later review our policy in light of this incident. School, church, sports, clubs, friends, and countless other activities consume almost every waking moment of our children's lives. Amidst these many good options there remains a crucial need for time to be together plus time to be by one's self. In this peer-dominated society, if parents do not set aside periods of time for these purposes, other more tantalizing options will squeeze them out altogether.

Sunday afternoon is one of the few blocks of time over which Dave and I still retain control. And since we believe it to be in everyone's best interest, we are unwilling to release this control. Even our best efforts to preserve this time are frequently thwarted. But we will continue to weigh each challenge for this cherished time against our guiding principle: the good of the family—collectively and individually.

"It is imperative that a family sense its own importance as a unit and that each member feel an intense sense of belonging within that unit," wrote Dr. David Lowry, headmaster of Brookside School at Cranbrook. "The family should be the most important grouping of which the child feels a part. The parents need to communicate clearly that they enjoy family life and that family membership is of highest priority."[4] Small decisions of each day repeatedly test those values we consider important to family living. Options seldom are black or white. Sometimes our decisions are wrong. But as the children watch us struggle with these very tensions, they will, I hope, come to recognize the importance we place on our family.

Family unity does not just happen. It begins by our articulating its importance and by our making decisions that endorse it. It is developed as we cultivate an interlocking network of loyalty, encouraging ties to the whole unit as well as to each individual. Such ties are strengthened by family participation at individual members' important events when possible, or by sending a representative when we can't all be present.

As the children get older, it becomes more necessary to plan carefully for time together as a family. Much of this can be gained by capitalizing on activities automatically built into daily rounds—eating, playing, working, riding. Mealtimes, for example, become valuable opportunities to discuss the day's activities or current events, to read a continued story, or to share a school report. Setting an attractive table, serving separate courses at a leisurely pace, monitoring the telephone—all these contribute to a heightened sense of occasion. But additional activities will disrupt these routines, making it necessary to schedule other special blocks of family time. Which particular time is irrelevant, as long as it is regularly scheduled and zealously guarded.

To experience its benefits, children need not understand

or even appreciate the value of this time. Children may prefer the exhilarating company of peers to the predictable presence of parents and siblings. Yet the family remains a constant refuge that serves to sustain them through the inevitable times when friends fail them. At any age peer pressure is easier to handle when you know that a loving core of people at home believe in you and will stand by you—no matter what.

The family bond, developed in one's early years by sharing confidences and experiences or celebrations and traditions, creates a strong sense of identity that influences one's personality and choices throughout life. Although most people will form other families in their adult years, the original family unit will provide a standard against which they can test personality traits and worldviews. This same family unit also provides in the deepest recesses of the heart a reservoir of support from which a member can draw.

The enduring significance of family relationships was brought home to me anew last Christmas when my brother called from his home in California. Although separated by nearly three thousand miles (and twenty years of living apart), we always touch base on this special day. After all, we spent our first twenty Christmases together. At the familiar sound of his voice, I realized that John gives me something no one else can. He, who shares my parents and my childhood, understands certain things as no other can. Although we once fought frequently, John helped me pioneer adolescence, advising me in both studies and relationships. When I was a young adult struggling with forming an identity apart from my family, no one knew better than he the difficulty of detaching from our parents who gave us so much that was good. Time and distance have not lessened this bond developed from common experience in our early years.

Family unity. How does it develop? Through numberless shared experiences: mealtimes, bedtimes, chores, celebrations, trials, and triumphs—year in and year out. Each common experience becomes a building block for the strong structure called family.

Relationships can't be legislated. There is no guarantee that grown children will maintain close ties with their parents or one another, but with deep commitment and conscious effort, parents can provide a strong family unit to support its members through their years at home and later on their independent journeys.

## YOUR STORY

1. Can you remember significant family times from your own childhood? What made them special to you?
2. What factors habitually discourage your family time together?
3. Upon what routine activities can you capitalize to create shared family experiences?
4. What blocks of time within the week can you most easily designate as "family time"?
5. What activities do you enjoy as a family? Plan ahead and set a "date" for a specified family event.

# THE GRACE OF COURTESY
## SHELTERING ELEMENTS OF
## CONSIDERATION AND LOVE

Dave and I return home from an evening engagement. The drapes are drawn, the windows closed, and doors locked as instructed. All is quiet on the home front. We note with satisfaction that the children are taking increased responsibility for themselves when we leave them on their own for an evening.

But upon entering our bedroom, we see a large sheet of paper propped against the bed pillow. The lengthy message is written in David's script:

> I don't know how to handle Jonathan. For the second night in a row he would not go to bed. After the TV program he stayed in the sitting room. I was going to read in the sitting room, but he wouldn't leave. So I went down to do my French and told him to go to bed. When I came back up at 9:25, he was still there. I was going to read, so I picked him up and brought him to his room. He would not go to bed and sat there with the lights on and finally went to sleep at 9:45. Then he got up again and wouldn't go to sleep and sat in the middle of his room. Then he played

games until 10:05. Help! (After I brought him to his room, I left him alone, did not say a thing, and of course took note.) P.S. When I turned out the lights he kept turning them back on and because I turned them back off he went into a tantrum and broke his pencil. So I left them on.

I'm torn between annoyance and amusement at my impassioned teenager who, resistant to writing a one-paragraph postcard, was moved to pen a full-page report about his brother's insubordination. This is but one in a series of journalistic forays since we acquiesced to an "in-family" baby-sitting service!

David is not the only reporter. On a scrap torn from a newspaper, Jonathan asserted: "David is being a brat. He about broke my knuckle with a toothbrush. He twisted my leg two times around and was standing on my stomach."

Kimberly also contributes to the chronicles, embellishing her complaints with an occasional footnote: "Please wake me up before breakfast so I can do my homework!! Probably around 6:15. Your Favorite Child!!! K. B. R."

Not every pillow message is militant. Some are merely informative: "I forgot to take my bath so I will take one in the morning. Jon." They may even be fraternal, showing mutual support against possible parental wrath: "I wanted to have a piggyback and so I got on David's back and he held me to drop me on Kimberly in the green chair and accsadently droped me on the basket and it's handel broke. I'm sorry. Jonathan" David added a P.S.: "He *is* sorry, too. (I hope you are in a good mood!)"

Regardless of subject, each note reflects the challenge of living in peace with others and the complexities of submitting the impulses, desires, and needs of one individual to the good of the group. Ideally, parents desire their children to resolve their conflicts on their own. (How often the crises recorded at night are forgotten by morning!) But to preserve an atmosphere of emotional safety, we must sometimes mediate or even discipline the guilty party.

The resolution of a given issue may not be as important as the greater lesson—learning how to get along with others. Through daily interaction, children discover what others do or do not accept in their behavior. They are forced to find ways to accommodate their wills to the needs and desires of others. In what better place can they learn survival skills and social graces than at home, where the zeal to get one's own way is tempered by the greater need to get along?

Courtesy, I'm convinced, is at the center of good relations. Here where the democratic ideal is so highly held, we easily dismiss *courtesy* as a quaint custom or define it narrowly in terms of "manners." But more careful consideration of its true meaning reveals a deeper message. *The Oxford English Dictionary* defines *courtesy* as a "graciously respectful" attitude toward "the position and feelings of others." Implicit in courtesy is an acknowledgment of rank (the hierarchy in one's family, vocation, or society) and the awareness of one's proper place in the scheme of things. Courtesy honors the feelings of others despite their rank and tacitly acknowledges that other people do matter. True courtesy is never reserved only for moments of personal advantage. Rather, it is that quality of character that informs one how to achieve proper relationships at all times.

In our homes we parents would do well to cultivate those courtesies that communicate one's respect for the positions and feelings of others. Rising when a "superior" enters a room, opening a door, or holding a chair—all are gestures that convey a deeper message of respect for others.

# THE GRACE OF COURTESY

The simple phrases *Excuse me, Thank you,* or *How do you do?* transcend mere convention. They express thoughtful concern for another's welfare.

Child psychologist James Dobson says that children must be taught courtesy. Home, among one's most beloved assortment of people, is the logical place for providing basic instruction. Simple rules of etiquette serve to check careless thoughtlessness toward family members who can so easily be taken for granted. Courtesy can sustain relationships when feelings of love falter or fail us.

The British novelist Charles Williams spoke of courtesy as a function of grace: "A kind of heavenly largesse of behavior—a flowing beneficence which souls in grace can *afford* to extend, because they have been given to so abundantly."[5] Courtesy, then, is no less than an image of grace at work.

In the words of Hilaire Belloc:

> Of courtesy, it is much less
> Than courage of heart or holiness
> Yet in my walks it seems to me
> That the Grace of God is in courtesy.

All conventions of manners and etiquette, from the most elaborate rules of court to the most practical reductions of the revised *Emily Post's Etiquette,* could be condensed in spirit to one simple guideline: "Do to others what you would have them do to you" (Matt. 7:12). While rules of etiquette can break down or judicial laws can be dismissed in a technicality, the golden rule of love transcends all legality—domestic or social.

Establishing and enforcing domestic policy will always challenge parents. To make our homes places of refuge

CHAPTER 2

where individual rights are protected and where people can drop their defensive guard, we must be ever vigilant. Kimberly recently reminded me of this during one sustained siege of brotherly teasing. She suddenly protested, "I thought this was supposed to be a safe place." But we must refrain from becoming so embroiled in the mechanics of mediation that we lose sight of a higher goal: instilling in children the "grace of courtesy"—the outward manifestation of an inner force of love.

## YOUR STORY

1. Define *courtesy*. Does it seem like a quaint or obsolete concept?
2. What is the relationship between courtesy and love?
3. What at-home courtesies are realistic to expect from your children? Teenage children? Adults? What courtesies would you like extended to you?
4. How can you most effectively instruct your children in common courtesy to other family members?
5. What are you currently doing to encourage loving relationships within the family unit?

# OPEN DOORS TO COMMUNICATION
## SHELTERING ELEMENTS OF
## SENSITIVITY AND ACCEPTANCE

"How did school go today?"

Kimberly drops her books on the car seat next to me and starts to answer my question. "Well . . . first period, nothing special." She shuts the door behind her and continues, "Second period we had a test. I think I did okay. . . ."

"You forgot to hang up your towel this morning," I insert.

"No I didn't."

"Yes, you did. I hung it up myself. It was wet—and on your carpet."

"Sorry. Well, anyway, third period Mr. Bates . . ."

"Kim, don't bite your nails," I chide spontaneously. "Go on. What were you saying about Mr. Bates?"

"Nothing."

"You were talking about your history class."

Silence. Kimberly stares straight ahead.

"C'mon Kim. What were you saying about Mr. Bates?"

"Mom," she answers at last, "I don't feel like talking anymore."

Slam. The door of communication is tightly shut

between us. While moments ago I had taken for granted the easy exchange of the day's events, now a team of horses can't force a word from my mute companion, silenced by my thoughtless nagging.

Oh, how I value open communication with my children! Yet how easy it is to stifle confidences with careless insensitivity! My very endeavors to encourage conversation can serve to block their expression, if I interrupt with the wrong opinion or reaction.

My failures in this area have convinced me that listening is an art that demands one's total concentration and careful cultivation.

Like any art, listening requires discernment and skill achieved through continual application. It requires the insight to permit your children to express themselves in their own time and their own way. How easy it is to react prematurely to a child's emotional statement. Listening demands the wisdom to recognize when you need to be silent to permit a child to verbalize thoughts or when a pertinent question might stimulate discussion. Listening requires the self-discipline to attend to the child's spoken and unspoken messages and to convey an effective response. When Jonathan insisted that "my teacher doesn't like me," our immediate response was to resist and challenge him. But Dave and I could help him with his classroom problem only when we asked him why he felt that way.

An atmosphere of acceptance is, of course, required to achieve communication. Scott Peck has said, "An essential part of true listening is the . . . setting aside of one's own prejudices, frames of references, and desires so as to experience as far as possible the speaker's world from the inside, stepping inside his or her shoes."[6]

Through the years we have come to recognize a distinct

pattern of communication with each child. "How did your day go?" normally elicits from Kimberly a detailed description of each memorable event. The same question produces only a grunt from David. When he is ready to talk, however, nothing will stop him.

Specific circumstances can usually open the door to good communication. Both Dave and I create special occasions with each child individually to encourage conversation. But frequently the most meaningful exchanges come at the most unexpected times: in the car to or from school, while washing dishes, or following a heated debate. How many other opportunities have we missed, due to our hurried schedules or cluttered minds?

As the children grow older, I see that the more I open my life to them, the more likely they are to open their lives to me. The more vulnerable I am in expressing my thoughts, feelings, and shortcomings, the more they confide theirs to me.

Ideally, communication is a two-way door. If demands are great, rewards are even greater. As we listen to one another, we come to know better the person hidden beneath the surface. As we exchange points of view, we come to understand the other's perspective and gain insight into the complexity of life. By giving another the time and attention required to solve problems and share triumphs, we tangibly demonstrate our love.

I hope Kimberly's silence will be short-lived. In any case it serves to provide a vital reminder: A child's confidence—even in the most trivial matters—is a precious, fragile trust to be tenderly cultivated and cherished. The doors of communication must be opened by my care and candor and kept open through sensitivity and wisdom.

# CHAPTER 2

## YOUR STORY

1. Do you know someone who is an exceptionally good listener? What characterizes this person?
2. In what situations is your child most likely to share thoughts freely?
3. How can you create a positive atmosphere for communication?
4. What are your greatest failings as a listener? Your greatest strengths?

# A TIME TO CELEBRATE SHELTERING ELEMENTS OF FAMILY TRADITION

As Dave goes upstairs I sink into the red chair, determined to prolong the loveliness of the evening. Tiny white lights spaced over the limbs of the Scotch pine shed a soft glow across the living room. The scent of gingerbread mingles with the fragrance of evergreen. Lilting boy-soprano voices of the King's College Choir soar from the stereo in sweet refrain, "O Come Let Us Adore Him."

A crush of red paper napkins and empty punch cups are the remnants of our family tree-trimming party—the climax of the week's decorating endeavors. We've festooned brass wall-sconces with ivy and plaid taffeta ribbon. We've draped garlands of evergreen from the mantel and wrapped them around the stairway banisters. Two miniature carolers standing outside an illuminated church set on top of the piano, invite us to sing from the book of carols open on the music rack. Our treasured olive-wood crèche adorns the mantel, where sheep, shepherds, camels, and wise men huddle around the sheltering stable.

The stage is set for our Advent activities and events. It's time to purchase, package, and mail presents for distant loved ones. Then we will write cards as we bake our ever-growing list of favorite Christmas goodies and our gingerbread house. Then we'll begin countdown to Christmas, as school programs, neighborhood parties, family shopping, and the church pageant crowd the calendar—not to mention countless unplanned events and frantic last-minute preparations.

On Christmas Eve our family will join the church family for the candlelight communion service, followed by punch and cookies with friends invited home. On Christmas Day we'll faithfully follow traditions developed through the years: children emptying their stockings at dawn; a festive brunch followed by the ceremonial opening of presents; our escape to Bok Tower Gardens for a carillon Christmas recital; our return home to our turkey dinner.

But now as I anticipate this Advent drama, I realize that each activity, each tradition (however special) represents sacrifice of time, energy, and sometimes money. How can we fit the additional activities into an already overcrowded schedule? Will the work be completed? Will our limited budget suffice?

Do the results of time-honored traditions merit the effort? When my irritability and weariness seem to equal the intended pleasure, when the family resists or takes for granted the very activities I've planned for them, the question is real. Its answer must transcend my fluctuating emotions.

Traditions unite families in bonds of love and caring. Each tradition, with its own ritual, is a link to one's past. Each shared activity is an affirmation of the bond we call family. Dr. James Dobson has said:

> The great value of traditions comes as they give the family a sense of identity, a belongingness. All of us desperately need to feel that we are not just a

cluster of people living together in a house but we're a family that's conscious of the uniqueness, its personality, character and heritage, and that our special relationship of love and companionship make us a unit with identity and personality.[7]

Traditions provide a vehicle by which we can say "I love you." Traditional family activities lure us from our increasingly independent schedules back into a circle of caring. Choosing appropriate holiday gifts requires thoughtful consideration for another's needs and desires. When we do things both with and for another, we convey the message that is so easily obscured by routine busyness: You matter. You are important to me.

Traditions offer some stability and direction in our rudderless society. Christmas, rich with significance, provides a delightful means for teaching fundamental beliefs and values. As we review biblical events and personalities, listen to carols researching seasonal symbols, read legends and stories that capture the spirit of Advent, the message and mood of Christmas imprints its truth into our minds and hearts.

Although the Advent season tops our list of sacred celebrations, the year's calendar is jeweled with other holy days and holidays—each with its beneficial rituals and celebrations. Each year is figuratively anchored by seasonal and liturgical events. The natural year has its rhythms of changing earth, sky, and sea, which provide countless opportunities to celebrate God's handiwork. The Christian year, with its cycle of seasons and festivals, provides numerous opportunities to underscore the revelation of God's Word.

To my delight, as the children get older they gain an

appreciation and anticipation of these traditional celebrations. Teenage David may flash a patronizing grin when I announce a new season with a telltale bulletin board, yet he was the first to challenge a threatened tradition: "What? No Easter egg hunt? We *always* hunt eggs after the sunrise service." As we yearly celebrate the repeating cycle of seasons, our children become increasingly involved in the preparations. Their "let's celebrate" stance extends beyond anything planned to something truly spontaneous: a good report card, the end of a school week, a change in weather.

The traditions we celebrate today are deposits in our bank of memories from which we can draw for the rest of our lives. Who can say when such a memory might warm a lonely heart or sustain one through some difficult time? Past memories provide lasting joy and strength.

Is Advent season with all its customs and celebrations worth my effort? Sitting in the glow of the Christmas tree and basking in the pleasure of the evening's festivity, I avow yes! Remembering seasons of my own childhood, I also affirm yes! In the busy days to follow, when my objectivity will be clouded by weariness and stress, I shall draw upon these tree-trimming reveries to remind myself, "Yes! Yes, it *is* worth it!"

Dear Lord, it is so peaceful, so lovely in our home, adorned for Christmas. May I carry the beauty of this moment into the rush and stress of the Advent season. Give me a gentle spirit. May my presence not contradict the very atmosphere I'm attempting to create for my family. And may the light of this moment guide me through this season in which we celebrate the Light who came to illuminate our darkness. Amen.

# A TIME TO CELEBRATE

## YOUR STORY

1. What special traditions did your childhood family observe?
2. Which of these are you observing in your present family unit?
3. What value do you see in family traditions?
4. What new traditions are you creating for your family?
5. What discourages you from creating and observing traditions?
6. Develop your own family resource library of celebrations of holidays and holy days.

# REACHING OUT
## SHELTERING ELEMENTS
## OF GIVING BEYOND

David sits on the porch rocker, staring straight ahead as he absorbs the shocking news of the divorce of close family friends.

"You know, Mom," he finally says, "with some families it doesn't really shock you—even if you didn't know there were problems. But with them—well, I couldn't be more surprised, even if Dad left us."

I wonder what can be behind that statement. Is he afraid? If it happened to them, could it happen to us? Or is it simply the statement of grim reality?

Reeling, myself, from the personal impact of this reality behind impersonal statistics, I consider the disintegration of this one family. They, like us, had invested richly in family living. All those things we value—loyalty, open communication, the balance between love and discipline, time together—they also demonstrated. Now the decision of one member to "find happiness elsewhere" has shattered the partnership of almost two decades.

Here with my son, deeply sobered by this devastating news, I'm reminded anew that the family should not— indeed cannot—be the only reason for one's existence. As important as it is for the strength of society and the security of the individual, the family is an inadequate basis for achieving personal happiness: There are no guarantees against death, disillusionment, divorce, or domestic disaster of any kind.

When the family unit is the end or only reason for one's existence, the family (and the individual) becomes ingrown and stagnant. I see parallels in the physical world. A body of water that has an inlet but no outlet becomes a rancid cesspool.

A family serves an invaluable function in nurturing the individual. It provides a stable, corporate base from which members can enter the world as well as a place where one can withdraw to recover personal identity when social tasks are accomplished. But as important as the family is to both individual and society, it was never intended to be the center of our existence. It is too fragile, too limited. "Wives, husbands, children make good 'spokes' but weak 'hubs,'" warned the Christian Medical Society.[8]

How, then, do we attend to the consuming occupation of fortifying the family without losing our larger perspective? How do we attend to the endless tasks required to build this basic unit without allowing it to become our entire focus or reason for being? I see the answer in a family's common vision and effort for something greater than itself—having a mission beyond the walls of home. Sociological studies confirm that when an individual is given a cause beyond personal survival, attainment of the cause not only mobilizes the person's resources, it also orders his or her most basic functions.

This ordering begins at home in one's earliest years, when one must accommodate other family members. It is strengthened as one learns to give from one's own personal resources, be it a cherished possession or a comforting hug.

# CHAPTER 2

One of Jonathan's finest moments occurred several years ago on the anniversary of Kimberly's birthday. He stuffed his entire savings into my hand and said, "Buy Kimberly the best stationery you can find."

As Kimberly opened her presents that evening, Jonathan danced around the table singing, "Birthdays are fun—even if they're not your own!"

Caring must widen in concentric circles to reach out to meet needs of one's immediate neighborhood, community, and church fellowship. In countless ways parents can collaborate with children to help them reach beyond the family: delivering flowers or cards to shut-ins, contributing clothing or toys to other children, or making cookies or valentines for elderly neighbors.

Caring should continue beyond one's immediate range of vision by raising family consciousness to global concerns. We do this through information, pictures, and specific prayer commitments. Whether we keep a bread bank at our table to alleviate world hunger or support an orphan overseas or write a letter to a congressman or missionary, we must do something: Just because we can't do everything doesn't mean we can't do anything.

As we reach out, we not only obey God's second greatest commandment, we experience another great spiritual law in action: The more we give to others, the more we receive ourselves. When we are united as a family in service, we become more closely bound to one another. When we focus on other people, the family falls into correct position. Personal and family problems take on a different perspective when one has less time to worry about them.

Even if it could guarantee exemption from domestic disaster or disappointment, the family, as we now enjoy it, is limited both in purpose and in duration. The awareness that our children are guests and not permanent residents helps us parents correct any tendency we may have to make the family our chief end. And involvement in the world beyond the boundaries of home better prepares our children to find their eventual places in that world.

So, then, let us build our shelters. Let us reinforce our roofs and outer walls—to nurture, strengthen, and protect our families. But let us never lose sight of the yet greater goal: to build a strong unified base from which individually and corporately we can reach out in love and service beyond the four walls of home!

## YOUR STORY

1. As important as the family unit is to society and to the individual, why is it an inadequate "hub" for our lives?
2. What are you doing to encourage caring and compassion for family members within the home? Neighborhood? Community? Church fellowship? World?
3. Why is it important to develop a sense of mission beyond the walls of your home?
4. Where do you turn for support when your family seems inadequate?

# CHAPTER 3
# WALLS: DELINEATION OF
# SPACE AND PLACE

*An architect specifies interior
partitions to accommodate different
functions and relationships plus
transitions from one activity to
another. A homemaker must provide
a physical environment that
accommodates the diverse activities
and personalities of each individual
while preserving the sanctity of the
forms and functions that undergird
the household.*

# RESONANCE OF ROOMS

*The forms and functions that undergird the household include individuality and interdependency, solitude and sociality, work and leisure.*

I'm alone in the house, the rooms are momentarily empty of people—and yet they are not really empty, resonating, as it were, with the lingering refrains of family living.

From my strategic position on the fireside chair, I can view the main passageways and partitions that designate the geometry of our home's first floor. Seen from my perch, each room echoes with its own particular melodies.

The dining room, which adjoins the living room through French double doors, still resounds with holiday and special occasions when friends and family linger around its oval table, talking and laughing long after the meal is finished. The iron candelabra overhead has illumined countless festive celebrations as well as common family suppers, dignifying every occasion with its soft radiance.

The morning room, in partial view through the French doors on each side of the breakfront, reverberates with its song of warmth and intimacy—the site of early morning solitude and late night conversations. As a little nest, with a cozy seating arrangement and a book-lined wall, the morning room begs one to come in, sit down, and settle into a good book or lively conversation!

A peep of blue, visible through a doorway on the east

93

wall of the dining room, evokes a cacophony of kitchen sounds. The kitchen is the undisputed heart of the home. Here melodies of cooking, eating, and cleaning mix (sometimes clash) with countermelodies of studying and tinkering or entering and leaving.

Through another doorway on the same wall, I see the generous hallway where my typewriter rests on a large table. I recall the hum of creativity echoing from its walls replete with chalkboard, bulletin boards, and brightly colored frames of our children's art.

The stair landing at the far end of the living room marks the transition from communal activity to private domain. The stairs leading up to the bedrooms and sitting room whisper of solitude and rest—solo voices in contrast to a chorus.

Even unoccupied, each room resonates with memories and significance. Each accommodates specific functions or dignifies—even transcends—its designated use through its particular form and procedures. Such is the character of rooms.

Consider the living room—space designed specifically for people to be together. The front door opens to this room. We've arranged the sofa, chairs, and tables into a conversational area, encouraging people to gather here to talk, relax, and enjoy one another. We've grouped the piano and other musical instruments at the far end of the room, likewise to encourage occupants to do something in a group. The message rings clear: "Here is a place to be at home— *together*."

Yet this room indicates even more. It reveals our feelings about activities we do together and the value we place on them. This is not a room set apart like parlors of old. An intimate arrangement of furniture dressed in jewel-colored fabrics suggests a comfortable coziness with a hint of royalty. Common everyday activities are here dressed up a bit, suggesting sovereignty beneath common working clothes or, in Emerson's words, "a king in disguise."

So it is with each room in the house: Partitions designate spaces for various functions. They also dignify each space by elevating these functions with specific forms and by imbuing a particular activity with deeper meaning. As one writer attested, "By distinguishing between one activity and another in a household, and by illuminating that distinction by such aids as customs and furniture and architecture, we clarify and hence dignify the whole enterprise."[1]

A meal might be most easily served from the counter where it was prepared, but to create an occasion we remove it from the place of its preparation. A case could be made for the placement of a sink and toilet next to a bed, but by separating these activities we at once define and dignify functions.

The functional and symbolic significance of rooms is universally acknowledged. The hearth as the innermost core of the general gathering place, for example, has been reinterpreted by generations of builders. English architect Baille Scott wrote, "a house, however warm, without a fire may be compared to a summer day without the sun."[2] Ancient Anasazi Indians underscored the symbolic aspect of their doorways by designing small entryways to remind them of passing from one space to another—making a transition. "Few things are indeed so strange as this thaumaturgic art of the builder," continued Scott. "He places stones in certain positions—cuts them in certain ways, and behold, they begin to speak with tongues—a language of their own, with meanings too deep for words."[3]

# CHAPTER 3

Frank Lloyd Wright's interpretation of the human dwelling is considered by many to be one of the most significant achievements in the history of modern architecture. Wright's "destruction of the box" and the resulting "free plan" broke with the conventional use of passages and enclosed spaces. And yet, according to Christian Norberg-Schulz, dean of the Institute of Architecture at the University of Oslo, during following developments "the free plan degenerated into a kind of general unidentified openness, making alienation rather than freedom manifest. Thus we recognize the eternal need for spatial figures which tell us where we are."[4] Or, as one frustrated "free plan" dweller protested, "What I need is *many* rooms, each with a function. No loft living for me—open plan living to me is confining. I need doors, walls, cubicles, enclosures."

Whether we prefer the open plan or enclosed spaces, the challenge remains the same: to provide spaces and places that successfully accommodate the wide diversity of functions for the broad range of needs of each dweller—spaces to eat, sleep, work, and play; places for adults and children of various ages, temperaments, and interests to be together and to be alone.

The original meaning of the word *room* was "place." Writer Thomas Frederick Davies has connected it with its Latin root *locus* meaning "open country." "Here, then," continued Davies, "is a liberating fancy. Every room is new territory to be explored, a bit of strange country to be discovered, a land of infinite possibilities to be visited and dwelt in."[5] Here, then, is open country to stake and settle with the infinite possibilities of human ingenuity and love. Rooms are the hallowed spaces in which the sacred mysteries of everyday living are enacted and elevated. Thus my calling is a high one: to create and celebrate the rites of household within these hallowed walls!

## YOUR STORY

1. What is your favorite room in your house? Why?
2. Consider the functions of each room. What functions are being most adequately served through your present partitions?
3. If you could add another room to your present dwelling, what would it be? Why?
4. In what ways could you make your present dwelling serve your family's needs more effectively?

# A ROOM OF ONE'S OWN
## SANCTITY OF PERSONAL SPACE

"Jonathan," I call from outside his bedroom door.

"Jonathan!" I knock. "May I come in?"

No answer.

I change my approach with a warning: "Honey, I'm coming in."

Silence. Cracking the door open slowly, I spot Jonathan sprawled across his bed, one arm flung across his teddy.

"Why don't you come on down and join us for dessert?"

The sensitive lad who minutes ago left the table in tears, is still smarting from his father's sharp rebuke. Aside from sniffles, I hear no sound from Jonathan.

My impulse to rush in and scoop up the little mourner is restrained by the memory of a small dormer bedroom, my refuge in the Cape Cod home of my childhood. There I sought solace from the cruel world until I regained my perspective and enough dignity to permit my entry back into normal society.

The pattern rarely varied. When rebuked for some misdemeanor, I would cry, protest, then dramatically retreat up the stairs to my bedroom. I would slam the door and fling myself across the bed, sobbing out my woes. When my emotions were finally spent, I would review the scenario with self-righteous indignation. *I will never come out of this room again—even if they beg me!* I would imagine how my parents would feel if I died. *Then they'll be sorry for the way they treated me, but it will be too late!* Comforted by these thoughts, my gaze would stray to my surroundings. I'd study the pattern of roses and vines on the papered walls or observe treetop branches brushing against the window panes. I'd look around the room at my doll collection and at objects displayed on the bureau. I would slip from my bed to my dollhouse, where I would lose myself in a private world of miniatures enlivened by my imagination. Then it was only a matter of time before I would trade my lonely play for some real companionship!

In her autobiography Mary Ellen Chase related her childhood longing for a room of her own within a household of four children where the bedroom "was a place to sleep in, not to escape to or enjoy." When her request to occupy a tiny room off the kitchen was at last granted, she took the key from her father and slipped it into her pocket. Feeling its cool hardness in her hand, she became aware that this key was far more than a tool to open a door. Decades later she observed, "Among the many evidences of understanding shown by modern young parents in bringing up their children, none is more wise than the allotment to a child, whenever possible, of a room of his own . . . however small, his own four walls within which he may keep his own possessions and treasures, bear his own humiliation and punishments, dream his own dreams."[6]

Whether or not one has the luxury of a private room, everyone needs some space to call his or her own. This is even true in the animal kingdom. Zoologist Professor Portmann of Basel, Switzerland, has observed that sea gulls perched on a quayside railing always stay no less than twelve inches apart. If another gull lights down closer, the one already perched will fly away at once. The law is universal: Each has a right to minimum living space. The German word that expresses this concept is *lebensraum*—room in which to live.

Space is not only required to recover from life's emotional skirmishes; it helps us separate one experience from another. Occasionally one needs to withdraw from the endless sequence of activities and find breathing space in which to absorb or savor the significance of events. Action, objects, words—each has greater clarity and significance when set apart from another.

We need room, also, to be alone with ourselves to keep in touch with our own thoughts and feelings, to dream our dreams, to pursue our interests, to know ourselves in relation to our Creator.

We parents must provide and honor privacy for each member of our family. Children can be particularly adept at finding their corner, cupboard, drawer, or "room to call their own." Likewise, adults should create space for themselves, whether it be a specific room designed for the purpose or a chosen corner that conveys the message "Private. Do Not Disturb."

A room of one's own with its lock and a key—people who have such a secure haven offer more to others and are likely to open the door beckoning others to come in.

## YOUR STORY

1. Where did you go as a child to be alone? Why did you choose this place?
2. Where in your home do you now seek solitude?

3. Pascal wrote, "All the unhappiness of men arises from one single fact, that they cannot stay quiet in their own room." Why is solitude so essential to our personal well-being?
4. Most of us cannot offer each family member "a room of one's own." What provision are you making for each individual to have private space?

# HUB OF THE HOUSE
# SANCTITY OF WORK

"It's David's turn to clear the table," Jonathan announces.

"Oh, no! I did it *last* night," David insists.

"All right," I interrupt, "you load the dishwasher while Jonathan clears the table."

"In that case *I'll* clear the table," David changes his mind.

"No, it's your turn to load the dishwasher, David," I insist.

"What about Kimberly? She's not doing *anything!*"

"She did the dishes last night. Come on, let's get moving. You need to get the table clear for homework."

Resigned, the boys go about their kitchen duties while Kimberly settles in at her homework assignments. I put out the ironing board and tackle a mound of clothing that has been piling up for several weeks. Dave walks into the room in response to the persistent ringing of the phone.

Without a doubt, the hub of our home is the kitchen. It is the centrifugal force around which the household spins. Here we cook, clean, and concoct all manner of goodies. Here we craft holidays, struggle over homework, conceive projects, and exchange daily events. Our kitchen is a gathering place, a core of creativity, our center stage for family living.

This homey room, inspired by the provincial European kitchens of my childhood fairy tales, is rooted in an aesthetic ideal and in sentiment. It is a composite of old and new, pleasing and practical. Through the years its surfaces and spaces gradually have filled with trinkets and treasures— children's art projects, delft china, Dutch tiles with hand-painted flowers, disks of stained glass, pewter, pottery, woven baskets, framed pictures, even a faded old quilt.

Though styled with Old World charm and sentimentality, the kitchen has a deeper significance. It is symbolic of service. Here, in a stream of endless days, I perform the repetitious and sometimes tedious task of preparing food and setting tables only to clear away the empty vessels, wash them, put them away, and then repeat the cycle. I wash, sort, and fold clothing that will only be dirtied again to be washed, sorted, and folded. . . . Each day I shake tablecloth and rugs, mop floors and countertops, only to repeat the task again tomorrow . . . and beyond.

And yet, the kitchen as a symbol of service is in one sense my salvation. It saves me from ultimate boredom through self-indulgence. "The enjoyment of leisure would be nothing if we had only leisure," wrote Elisabeth Elliot. "It is the joy of work well done that enables us to enjoy rest, just as it is the experiences of hunger and thirst that make food and drink such pleasures."[7]

Fourteenth-century Chaucer stated a twentieth-century psychological principle with these simple words, "Great peace is found in little busy-ness." How many times have my humble daily tasks taken my brooding mind off things that bound me? As I turn my thoughts to others through these small acts of love, I am saved from myself. The kitchen is a crucible purging the dross from self with the fiery heat of service.

Scripture elevates work to an even higher plane, asserting that it can be sanctified by one's motive. "Whatever you do, work at it with all your heart, as working for the Lord, not for men" (Col. 3:23). When labor is consecrated to God, everything from the most ordinary duty to the most sublime expression of creativity becomes an act of worship. When work transcends its mundane function, it becomes a song of praise, a work of art.

This is not to deny that certain occupations have greater appeal than others. Writing exhilarates me in a way that washing dishes cannot. I can't help but pity the individual who, while desiring one vocation, is saddled with another. But if personal worth rests on a particular task, then I and countless others are in trouble. Even the most glorious profession may have dreary aspects. One's vision must see beyond the nitty-gritty of duty!

A tale is told of three men working in a stone yard. A passerby asked, "What are you doing?"

"I'm earning my bread," said the first.

"I'm following my trade," said the second.

"I'm building a cathedral," said the third.

Which am I doing: cleaning house, making meals, supervising children? Or am I creating a home, shaping lives, and supporting the calling of my husband? Am I cutting stones or building a cathedral?

Admittedly, I frequently allow dull chores to obscure this high calling. But when lucid, I gain a perspective on my work that is of far greater value than the details of each task.

Above the butcher-block counter in the work area of my kitchen is a single row of delft tiles. Centered on the window mullion above the kitchen sink, one special tile commemorates with a Scripture verse the date we moved to this house: "As for me and my house, we will serve the Lord" (Josh. 24:15 KJV). Each member of this household must determine individually how to serve the Lord. But as for me—how do I serve? I serve Him by cleaning and cooking or washing and ironing. I serve Him in my kitchen, or in any place where I might faithfully and lovingly perform those tasks set before me.

## YOUR STORY

1. Where is the center of work in your home?
2. What household tasks do you most enjoy?
3. What household tasks do you least enjoy? What difference would it make if you actively worked as if you were working for Jesus?

# THE NEST
## SANCTITY OF INTIMACY

"Where shall we have our tea party, Jonathan?" I inquire, pausing in the kitchen doorway carrying a silver tray laden with demitasse cups, a porcelain teapot, and a plate of cookies.

"In the morning room, of course," he replies without hesitation. "It's my favorite room."

Setting the tray on the tea table, I locate our place in the book we're reading together, while Jonathan pours lemonade into our tea cups.

"Why is the morning room your favorite?" I continue as we nibble on shortbread cookies.

"Because it's so cozy. And I like the way it's filled with all sorts of neat things." He points around the room.

"I know what you mean," I respond, gazing about the tiny space crowded with oversized furniture and cluttered with favorite books, pictures, and memorabilia.

I consider the development of this little room from pastor's study to morning room. From the beginning, I fear its color and fabric choices were influenced by pictures of English country homes with their intimate morning rooms swathed in faded chintzes and old lace. But my intentions for making this a study room for Dave were honorable when I

106

selected a comfortable armchair for the "pastor" and had one wall lined with shelves for his library. Granted, the dainty writing desk and tea table added distinctly feminine elements—but what else could one use in such a small space?

It wasn't long before my favorite pictures and photos, boxes, and bibelots were spread out on open surfaces. Shelves filled up with my own beloved volumes and with sourcebooks for the children. The desk soon harbored my planning calendar, stationery, letter rack, and other personal effects. (After all, it was much more sensible for the pastor to work one block away in his roomy church study, with his theological library at arm's length, than here at home!)

As the room filled with familiar things, more people gravitated to this corner of the house. Before fixing breakfast, I often prepare myself for my busy day in the quiet solitude of this room. When children leave for their respective schools, Dave and I here delight in a few moments together before launching into our separate schedules. Following supper, when Dave and I slip off to our little nest to share the day's events over a cup of coffee, the children invariably appear one by one, usually settling into these cramped quarters in preference to open territory of other larger rooms. Be it for social camaraderie or some solitary pursuit, the morning room has become a favored place in this house.

A cozy corner of an intimate room has universal appeal. Humans seem to have a need to withdraw into a special corner and be cradled in its embrace. "Intimacy needs the heart of a nest,"[8] maintained Gaston Bachelard. For achieving coziness, intimacy, or just plain convenience, the cradle aspects of a small room are hard to beat. Designer Mark Hampton extolled the many unique properties of small rooms, from Mr. Badger's storybook house to Louis XV's private apartments at Versailles, when he wrote, "The intimacy they achieve would not have been possible on a large scale. In their smallness they have a universal appeal that spans centuries."[9]

Designer Georg Anderson encourages his clients to create a snug, intimate place in their homes, whether it be a separate room or a corner of a larger room. He wrote, "From personal experience, I know that if you will use it as a personal sanctuary in which to seek and receive God's direction and blessing, as a place for quiet talks with other family members and as a place simply to be together, you will find an important source of spiritual strength."[10]

The room we originally set aside as the pastor's study has undergone an unexpected transformation. Yet its original function, to nourish and edify, to build up the pastor so that he in turn can bolster others, has never changed. This little nest of chintz, lace, well-worn books, and bibelots has served Dave as much as his desk, files, and theological tomes have.

## YOUR STORY

1. In what room of your house are family members most likely to congregate?
2. What makes this room attractive to them?
3. Most people do not have separate rooms for each household function. How could you create a cozy corner or intimate place to be together—or alone—within existing rooms?

# SALUTE TO THE OLD-FASHIONED FRONT PORCH
## SANCTITY OF LEISURE

"Creak, creak, creak." The rhythmic squeak of rockers accompanies our conversation as Dave and I sit on the front porch sipping lemonade.

"Watch this!" yells David, tossing a baseball high into the air for Jonathan to catch in his mitt.

"Good one," encourages his father. Back and forth the boys take turns throwing and catching the ball, perfecting their skills by ever-greater challenges.

The front door opens. Kimberly and her friend appear on the porch. "The cookies are ready," they announce.

The boys drop their mitts and ball and race to the house to claim their share of the bounty, slamming the door behind them.

Dave and I exchange bemused glances and settle back to enjoy the pleasure of the front porch. The evening air is still, balmy, and lightly scented with the fragrance of the tea olive blossoms. A chorus of crickets and frogs sounds off from the little lake across the street. Several ducks, having crossed the street, pick at our lawn. Biscuit observes the intruders, then with feline dignity abandons the lawn for the porch. Brushing against our ankles, he jumps onto my rocker and

CHAPTER 3

curls up in my lap with proprietorial smugness. Periodically Dave and I swat at mosquitoes humming about our heads.

From our front-row seats, we observe the passing parade. A couple of boys pedal by, precariously balancing their fishing poles and tackle boxes while steering their bikes. Cars pass. Occasionally a driver honks his horn and waves from his window. The melting sun tints the western sky with vibrant shades of pink.

"That's a welcome sight!" An unexpected voice breaks into our reveries—a neighbor walking her dog. "And far too rare," she adds with approval of our leisure.

Dave and I agree with her and lament the crowded schedule that usually precludes such a lazy evening. Our old-fashioned front porch offers these moments, but it is also evocative of an altogether alternative way of living. "I remember porches the way some people remember home-made ice cream or the big bands of the 1940s," reminisces JoAnn Barwick, editor of *House Beautiful*. "Porches are one of the nostalgic centers of my childhood, the focus around which so many summer memories were made."[11] Front porches suggest lazy afternoons in which you curl up on a swing with a good book; simple summer suppers; hours to fill with street gazing, chattering about trivia, or philosophizing about enormities while the evening air thickens with stars and night songs.

My earliest memories include summers at the lake. One ritual of each day—or so it seemed—was an after-dinner visit to my grandparents who were sitting on the screened porch of their wooden bungalow. We would settle into their wicker furniture to enjoy light refreshments. When the conversation progressed from an exchange of the day's events to weightier adult concerns, I would slip away to diversions, until "Why, it's dark already!" signaled the visit's end.

What has happened, one might wonder, to the "era of the front porch"—the cool, shady cloister of philosophers, that gathering-shed for conversation and matchless setting for charm, comfort, and romance?

The history of the American front porch is in microcosm a document of the social movement of our country. Originating in the South, porches grew in popularity throughout the country toward the turn of the century when the increasingly popular Victorian homes became almost wrapped in their spacious porches. The push to the suburbs, resulting from the housing boom of the early 1900s, likewise contributed to their zenith, as houses built on small lots faced their porches toward tree-lined streets.

The past several decades, however, witnessed a decline in the front porch of the new suburbia. The focus shifted from the sociability of the street to the privacy of the backyard. Action moved from the front porch to the backyard patio and screened porch, or inside to air-conditioned comfort in the den.

And yet now more and more new homes boast porches; those of older homes are being restored or refurbished. Contemporary architectural journals and decorating magazines are giving a nod to the simple, old-fashioned porch. Why, amidst the pressing realities of our fast-paced culture, is there a returning desire for the front porch?

I'm sure sheer sentiment is one reason: an effort to capture the romance of a seemingly simpler era. But there are also other reasons. A renewed appreciation for the best elements of the past—spiritually as well as materially—has caught the imagination of every level of society: well-crafted homes with old-fashioned charm; a transition from indoor to outdoor living; a way of life that combines the need for privacy with the pleasures of nature. "Whatever else they are," maintained Mark Hampton, "porches are box seats from which those of us who worship nature can relax and watch the show."[12]

For us reluctant creatures of our frantic generation, the front porch is a timely reminder of timeless values. Window boxes and wicker, hanging baskets and glider swings, rockers and clay flowerpots might not re-create the past with its nostalgic appeal of a slower pace and simpler pleasure, but the front porch offers a perpetual invitation to steal away with a good book, enjoy a supper "*alfresco*" with the family, watch day ease into night to the accompaniment of a chorus of frogs and crickets. I salute this wonderful American phenomenon—this buffer between house and yard, this outdoor parlor, this box seat before nature: the old-fashioned front porch.

## YOUR STORY

1. In what ways did your family enjoy leisure time when you were a child?
2. What elements of the past do you wish you could incorporate into your life today?
3. What aspects of your family's lifestyle jeopardize "leisure time" today? Realistically, what can you do to simplify your crowded schedule?
4. Given the rarity of the front porch today, what places in your home are most conducive to quiet relaxation? What can you do to encourage your family in leisurely pursuits such as reading, conversation, or the enjoyment of nature?

# TWO SOLITUDES: ONE SOLIDARITY
## SANCTITY OF MARRIAGE

"Your bedroom should be the most intimate and private room in the house," wrote Mark Hampton in his book *On Decorating*. "A result of all this delicious privacy is the freedom to gather around yourself all the trappings of personal comfort and luxury."[13]

Mentally I measure our master suite by Hampton's standard. Our bedroom and sitting room, separated by a small bathroom, are unified by its decorative theme—a garden bower carpeted and painted in Wedgwood green, accented with chalk-white woodwork and ceiling-to-floor Frenchvoile curtains. The personal touches, flower-patterned pillows on wicker furniture, linen table coverings, family pictures and memorabilia, favorite paintings, and books, bespeak the intimate luxuries and comforts of our private world.

Here in our treetop retreat, the separate lives of Dave and myself merge. Yet even as we come together in this place at the beginning and end of each day, there are clear indications of individuality: a paper napkin from a ladies' luncheon and a golf scorecard clutter a bookshelf; an end table is piled with decorating magazines and back issues of *Sports Illustrated*. Other concessions are evident: The television set clumsily intrudes into this ethereal sitting room in deference to the weekend's sports schedule.

The paradox of both separateness and solidarity in matrimony is also captured in three pieces of furniture: a desk, Dave's armchair, and our king-sized bed. My white wicker desk faces the windows on the west wall of our bedroom. Flanked by a bookstand on one side and a file cabinet on the other, it functions as a retreat from house-keeping activities and social interaction downstairs. For a life marked by endless physical and relational demands, my desk symbolizes the oasis of quiet reflection. Surrounded by my children captured in snapshots, I can engage in the elusive experience of locking ideas into words. At my desk I sift, sort, and file the many pieces of my fragmented life; I stretch and exercise my mind, which has become inundated with the trivialities of daily existence.

Dave, in direct contrast, regards his recliner as an escape from the enormities of ministry. It represents a temporary reprieve from his office desk—the center of his work at church—where he prepares sermons, studies, administers ecclesiastical business, and advises about the full range of human experiences. Here in the solitude of the sitting room he can relax with a periodical or crossword puzzle, even referee a television ball game.

The brass bed represents a coming together, not only in the physical union of marriage but in the merging of our separate lives at the end of each day's divergent activities. Together we begin and end the day. Here in the privacy of our bedroom, we relate and review individual experiences; we plan and coordinate family activities.

Beyond purely practical functions, these furnishings denote two concepts crucial to a healthy marriage. My desk and Dave's chair are symbols of the separateness vital to individual identity and growth. The more our lives become rich and satisfying—independent of each other, the more effectively we can each contribute to our marriage relationship. Our bed is a symbol of the solidarity that results from the union of two individuals bound by a loving commitment to their partnership. We strive consciously to resolve our differences, to build and strengthen our common bonds.

Twenty years of marriage have distilled my false expectations and romantic illusions through a filter of reality. Early in our marriage I sought to overlap our lives in every area, suffering through his sports activities (or feeling guilty when I wasn't) and subjecting Dave to my detailed accounts of teaching or mundane child care—all in the name of togetherness. Gradually I began to recognize the value of separate as well as overlapping interests. I discovered that personal space was not only healthy for us individually but also for our union.

Through the years we have enjoyed tremendous rewards resulting from our struggle to balance our separateness and solidarity. The children as well as the marriage partnership profit from our individual strength. The compromises required for solidarity have jolted us from ruts of thinking and forced us to stretch and grow so as to assimilate the personalities and preferences of the other.

At weddings Dave repeats a prayer that increases in meaning to me as I learn more of what is required from each partner to make marriage all God intended it to be. As the young couple kneels at the altar, my heart echoes Dave's "amen"—both for them and as a renewed commitment to our marriage.

Now make such assignment to them on the scroll of Your will that will bless them and develop their

characters as they walk together. Give them
enough tears to keep them tender, enough hurts to
keep them humane, enough failure to keep their
hands clenched tightly in Yours, and enough
success to make them sure they walk with God.

May they never take each other's love for granted.
When life is done and the sun is setting, may they
be found then, as now, still hand in hand, still
thanking God for each other. This we ask through
Jesus Christ, the Great Lover of our lives.
Amen.[14]

## YOUR STORY

1. What interests do you and your spouse cultivate
   independently from each other?
2. What areas of mutual enjoyment do you pursue?
3. What do you currently consider the greater need in
   your marriage: solidarity or separateness?
4. Often marriage partners experience opposite needs.
   Discuss your individual needs with each other.
   Strategize specific ways in which you can correct the
   perceived imbalances in your marriage.

# MORE THAN DINING
## SANCTITY OF HIERARCHY OF PLACE

"David, take off your cap," Dave instructs his son who, arriving late from baseball practice, joins us at the dining room table.

"I can't," he responds. "My hair is a mess."

"It doesn't matter. Your mother has gone to all this effort to prepare a special family meal; the least you can do is show basic respect."

"C'mon, Dad! It has nothing to do with respect!" David protests. "My hair is all sweaty and matted from practice. What difference does it make? It's just us."

"Yeah," chimes in Jonathan, eager to support his big brother's position and, perhaps, his own vested interest. "What difference *does* it make?"

Encouraged by the unsolicited support, David argues his point, Jonathan adding occasional comment. Kimberly follows the debate with silent interest.

"Off with the hat," Dave holds firm, unswayed by passion or logic.

David redirects his focus to me. "Mom, certainly you wouldn't be offended if I left my hat on. You've let me wear it at the table before," he adds, binding me to an unwritten rule of precedence.

# CHAPTER 3

"Off with the cap!" Dave commands with unrelenting consistency. "This is nonnegotiable."

David jerks his cap off his head and throws it to the ground. Acquiescent but not convinced, he launches into his meal continuing his case.

"Tell the truth, Mother. You know you've let me wear my baseball cap at meals before. As a matter of fact, I wore my cap yesterday evening, didn't I, Jonathan? I clearly remember coming home from practice, sitting down, and leaving my hat on."

"You could have. I guess it just seems to stand out more in the dining room."

I'm sure we have overlooked his crime of convention amidst the casual chaos of kitchen eating, but somehow the baseball cap seems more intrusive within this context: the candlelit table spread in linen, set with silver and china. The efforts taken to create such an atmosphere demand a corresponding response. What we might have overlooked by default in the kitchen, seems unacceptable in the dining room.

Places of dining not only inform our behavior but provide insight into a given culture's domestic history. Laura Ashley, in her *Book of Home Decorating,* observed that over the decades, as life became less formal and faster paced, rigorous protocol for mealtimes and places and table settings was gradually replaced by improvised interpretations. Today the formal dining room is frequently replaced by an informal kitchen gathering, a screen-porch picnic, or a backyard barbecue.

As much as I delight in the creative and practical possibilities of dining, I maintain a special appreciation for the unique attributes of a formal dining room and what it evokes from us. A dining room provides far more than a check for careless manners. It is a calm stopping place where family and friends can gather and relax away from household clatter. It offers me an added security: I can prepare the table ahead of time without inconveniencing my kitchen work. Then we can also enjoy the meal without the visible reminders of cooking and cleaning up. Both culinary and conversational contributions are somehow enhanced by lovely surroundings and a leisurely ambience.

In addition to its functional qualities, the dining room, like any other room, has its own symbolic significance. The oval walnut table encircled with bentwood chairs occupies center stage. The fixed seating arrangement represents our respective roles: Parents seated at opposite ends establish order and discipline; siblings seated in between learn fundamentals in courtesy by denying their immediate self-gratification for the good of all. Father, at the head of the table, represents the dominant voice of authority. We gain a more accurate sense of proportion from the elementary lessons of ordered living that we learn through manners and service at the table.

The boys' resistance this evening to a basic amenity reinforces for me the necessity to counter the current trend to downplay distinctions, to minimize accepted conventions. Parental inconsistency notwithstanding, formal dining provides an appropriate setting and the occasional opportunity to underscore the meaning behind the customs that have endured society's test: the survival of the fittest.

Subdued, if not convinced, David sits bareheaded, submitting to the fate of formal dining. His father and I chalk up one, small victory for the sanctity of spaces and the lessons of "place" implicit within their four walls.

# CHAPTER 3

## YOUR STORY

1. Name your favorite at-home dining place as a child. What made this place satisfying to you?
2. What were mealtimes like in your childhood home? Where did each person sit around the table? What was your favorite meal?
3. The interpersonal dynamics around the table are more important than where or what you eat. What characterizes the mealtime atmosphere in your home? What specific measures can you take to improve this significant family time (for example, setting specific times for meals, not answering the phone, enforcing or relaxing table manners)?
4. Consider ways in which you could enhance the functions of each room with increased efficiency, beauty, or rituals.

# CHAPTER 4
# ELEMENTS OF STYLE:
# DECORATION AND DESIGN

*An architect reveals a personal style through structural details and ornamentation. Likewise a homemaker expresses herself through the furnishing and decoration of her home.*

---

# WHAT IS STYLE?

*Elements of style reveal and affect
the inhabitants' values, preferences,
and personalities.*

What is style? Bookstores are stocked with sourcebooks describing the domestic styles of a given country or period of time. Lavish illustrations detail the traditional warmth and comfort of the English style, the elegant refinement of the French style, the domestic practicality of the Dutch style, or the clean, functional lines of the Scandinavian style. Others catalog the common characteristics of outstanding periods of domestic history: the ecclesiastical influences of the Middle Ages, eighteenth-century French rococo or English classical revivals, the neo-anything of the Victorian age, the stylish simplicity generated by the nineteenth-century arts and crafts movement, or the stark minimalism of the twentieth century.

As I examine the pictures and texts of these informative resources, I see that it's impossible to limit any region or age to a single style. Diversity abounds. Architectural and decorative features of one era spill over into another. At best, one can hope to capture the spirit of a place or time by describing its most characteristic features.

It is even more difficult to define what comprises a distinctive, individual sense of style. Russell Lynes, looking back over ten years of writing a monthly "Leisure and Style"

CHAPTER 4

feature for *Architectural Digest* magazine, observed, "I have no intention of being brash enough to define style or to say why some individuals have it, and others . . . do not. I couldn't do it ten years ago, and I cannot do it now."[1] Extravagance and current notions of "good taste" have nothing to do with style in people—or their houses.

Style is easier to describe than define. Three women come to mind when I think of style. Soon after our move to Michigan I was invited to a neighbor's home for tea. Greeting me at the door of her white clapboard house, my silver-haired hostess led me into a living room I remember well: Against a backdrop of silver-gray carpets and white walls, hung ceiling-to-floor curtains of hand-embroidered Swiss organdy. Antiques of dark polished wood and sparkling touches of cranberry glass accented the room. Through windows I could see flowers in window boxes and cutting gardens. My lingering impression was one of peace and serenity.

In contrast to the delicate refinement of my neighbor's home was the simple cedar house built by friends in anticipation of their retirement. "At this stage in our lives I'm trying to unclutter my existence," Anne said as she directed my attention to the wooden floors that she easily maintained by a quick sweep; she could shake the rag rugs onto her lawn. Their chairs and tables were carefully crafted and finished by her husband. Wildflowers and grasses, handmade shawls and quilts provided homey touches. Outside the kitchen door they'd planted a vegetable garden. Anne, with her timeless tweeds and cardigan sweaters and her short hair swept back off her face, seemed completely at one with her home: natural and straightforward.

Yet a third home exuded exuberance. The dominant impression in the home of the hostess of our book club was an abundance of flowers: fresh flowers in containers of all shapes and sizes, furniture upholstered in garlands of spring flowers, and bedroom floor painted buttercup yellow and stenciled with fanciful floral designs. She displayed a pair of French baker's racks trimmed in shiny brass; she'd spread several small round dining room tables with pretty pastel cloths. The total effect was as blithe and free-spirited as was our hostess, who delighted in taking us on the "tour of home."

Style? None of these homes conformed to a particular period of decorative history. None reflected a given country or region. But each of these homes had style. Each made its own distinct decorative statement. Each reflected beautifully the personality of its occupant. Together they inspired me, then a young and inexperienced homemaker, to do the best I could with whatever I had available to me.

What is style? Difficult though its meaning is to capture in words, architects and designers have through the years agreed on certain of its elements. Integrity of form is a fundamental component. "Be truthful in form and expression and the future will admire your work,"[2] challenged Finnish architect Eliel Saarinen in an address given to architects in 1931. A second universally accepted element of style is the unity of the composition of diverse decorative components. Yet integrity of form and unity of composition do not provide an adequate definition of style. We all have seen homes that adhere to principles of design and composition. We have witnessed picture-perfect interiors—faithful copies of period rooms, perhaps—but something was missing. Cold and lifeless, in their very perfection they lacked the personal touch, that individual signature of the inhabitant.

William Strunk, in his concise handbook for writers,

*The Elements of Style,* observed: "Style takes its final shape more from attitudes of mind than from principles of composition . . . Style *is* the writer, and therefore what a man is, rather than what he knows, will at last determine his style."[3] Frank Lloyd Wright applied this understanding of style to architecture: "Style *is* the man . . . Style develops from within."[4]

So it is with our homes: Style *is* the man or woman. It is the sum total of all that we bring of ourselves to our homes. "Home," wrote Barbara Ascher, "is the soul we wrap around ourselves, an outward display of inner selves. Aspiration, affectations, quirks, and passion, bits and pieces of the past—as it was or as we wished it to be—go on parade within those walls." Ascher then quotes Gloria Vanderbilt: "All decorating comes out of our deepest feelings about ourselves, about beauty, and about our hope for ourselves."[5] To formulate a personal style one should consider principles of design and composition; one should use accessible resources—natural and human. But that is only the starting point, the substance upon which you can work your own personal alchemy; synthesizing what you admire and desire with what you are and have. Stated in simple formula: Inspiration plus personal resources plus imagination equals style.

Few of us will realize materially our dream house. But each of us can apply this formula to the here-and-now of our domestic situations. We can take our dreams and desires, along with our skills and materials, and synthesize them into a unique decorative statement—our own personal style!

## YOUR STORY

1. Describe your favorite house. What elements hold the greatest appeal to you?

2. How does this house differ from your own home?
3. If you could design and decorate a home without financial restraint, what would it be like?
4. How does your present home reflect your values, interests, and personality? Do you feel your home "misrepresents" you in any way?

# DEVELOPING A PERSONAL STYLE
## ELEMENTS OF STYLE
## REFLECT THE HOMEMAKER

The story is told of a woman who waltzed into the studio of a famous designer and demanded something marvelous in a hat. The designer artfully twisted a bit of ribbon around a simple bonnet and held it up, a creation so restrained it shouted money and style. "I adore it," she cried.

"Very good," said the designer. "Three hundred dollars."

"What?" retorted the woman. "For *ribbon*?"

The designer whipped the ribbon out of the bonnet and laid it in her hand. "No, Madam," he said. "The ribbon is free."

The message of this anecdote is perfectly clear: She was paying for the *style*. Anyone confronted for the first time with the challenge of decorating a home knows only too well the value of that intangible ingredient called style. Such was my experience when as a young bride I arrived at our first apartment with a boxful of wedding gifts and a head full of dreams! The "bonnet and ribbon" of our first home consisted wholly of those wedding luxuries, cast-offs from friends, and whatever else we could salvage from second-hand stores. When it came to style, I knew only two things: what I *didn't* want and what we couldn't afford.

I grew to value one wedding gift, a *McCall's Decorating Book*. The prologue offered this encouraging perspective: "In decorating, one of the first requirements is to dig down into the unconscious and rediscover that buried childish curiosity and creativity, that fresh way of seeing things. Once found, it should be polished up and put into use again—because all design starts inside you, not outside."[6] Poring over the pages of this elaborately illustrated text, I made a liberating discovery: Anything goes! Rooms stunningly furnished in costly period pieces were accented with affordable charm: wildflowers bunched into teacups; candle holders of all shapes and sizes massed on mantels; walls hung with fabrics and objects of sentiment; windows draped with burlap and pillow ticking; tables spread with colorful sheets and quilts. Army trunks and apple crates served as end tables and bookcases.

We could not afford new furniture and accessories, but we could improvise with the "ribbon and straw" of our here and now. Purchasing only the most essential pieces of furniture, we pulled out our wedding gifts and family cast-offs, scrutinizing them for decorative possibilities. Dave and I scouted secondhand stores for cheap "finds." Our decorative statement was created from household items—books, plates, candle holders, containers, and fabrics hung on walls and draped over windows and tables. We thought it beautiful!

Through the years we've slowly acquired additional furnishings along with certain tricks of the trade. (Paint, we've learned, achieves the greatest effect for the least cost. And one fine piece of furniture can set the tone of an entire room.)

But it wasn't until we anticipated the move into our present home that I consciously began to think in terms of a definite style. Although I had no name for it, I knew what I liked and I filled a notebook with photographs of interiors, color chips, and fabric samples to illustrate my aesthetic ideal. Predominant were interiors of European country homes comfortably furnished with mellowed antique furniture, accessorized with heirloom silver, fine linens and porcelain, oriental carpets, and memorabilia accumulated over years, maybe centuries.

Influenced by this ideal, the new manse acquired a decidely Old World feeling. Dark glowing woods, cranberry-colored drapes, rich-patterned oriental style carpets, and ivory walls gave a distinctly English atmosphere to the living room. I lifted the sage-green and old-rose color scheme of the dining room and adjoining morning room right off the cover of *The Diary of an Edwardian Lady*. A Dutch influence is evident in the kitchen. Kimberly's room with its white painted furniture and enameled iron bed dressed with eyelet could have been transplanted from Laura Ashley's Welch farmhouse. I picked the lush accent colors of the master suite from Monet's provincial gardens.

Inspiration and compromise, synthesis and adaptation, trial and error—all were important aspects in the process of developing our personal style over two decades. What originated by necessity as merely eclectic has gradually evolved into an "Old World eclectic"—in its broadest sense.

More than conformity to any particular style, I want a home that embraces our family and friends with warmth and intimacy, a home that expresses our interests and personalities with integrity and beauty. I want a home furnished with love and memories, dreams and hopes—a home that is an autobiography of our family.

Looking back at our efforts to create a livable home out of limited resources, I recognize several guiding principles:

## DEVELOPING A PERSONAL STYLE

*Learn to see:* Develop an eye for what truly pleases and discover the possibilities for interpreting that vision with what you have or can afford. One friend transformed a large closet into a delightful sewing center, her design inspired by the colors of a painting that now hangs in the room. Interior designer John Stefanidi stores away sketches and photographs from his travels. He refers to them when he needs seed ideas for his own designs: The pattern of a Bukhara embroidery becomes a stenciled wall pattern, a Roman gallery inspires an ornate cupboard.

*Work with what you have:* Consider the possibilities inherent in the present environment. You may not be able to afford a matching set of furniture, but a fresh coat of paint applied to odds and ends can transform and unite diverse elements. A friend, daughter of missionaries, relates how her mother would transform their temporary dwelling in Vietnam, creating lavish centerpieces from native flowers. When all else fails, turn down the lights and light up the candles. Things look better by candlelight.

*Live now:* Don't wait for the dream house that may never materialize. Edith Schaeffer has lamented the mentality that fails to enjoy what it has while longing for what it idealizes.

Your home expresses *you* to other people, and they cannot see or feel your daydream of what you expect to make in that misty future, when all the circumstances are what you think they must be before you will find it worthwhile to start. You *have* started, whether you recognize that fact or not. We foolish mortals sometimes live through years of not realizing how short life is, and that TODAY *is* our life.[7]

131

# CHAPTER 4

Even the most temporary dwelling can be made attractive with a few decorative touches enriching the here and now of our everyday lives. Lesley Blanch claims that her nomadic years with husband Romain Gary, French writer and diplomat, taught her to "travel heavy," setting a "few favorite objects" around her, no matter where she unpacked to sleep a night. She carried a small icon, a teapot, a cushion, and a senna rug.[8] Whether you're living a nomadic existence in hotel rooms, a few months in a bachelor's flat, or temporarily in a rental home, you can create a more sympathetic environment by investing it with personal touches.

Developing a personal style: Straw and ribbon is the material we all have—to a lesser or greater degree. "Style" is one's own unique twist of the ribbon, developed and refined through experience—one's own personal signature!

## YOUR STORY

1. Describe the style of your childhood home. How has it influenced the style of your present home?
2. What prevents you from having your "dream house" now?
3. What influences do other family members have on the decor of your home?
4. Considering your present resources, what can you do to make your home a truer reflection of your family and yourself?

# A JOY FOREVER
## ELEMENTS OF STYLE AFFECT
## INHABITANTS

"A thing of beauty is a joy forever," wrote poet John Keats. Although one might challenge Keats's romantic concept of beauty, his praise is due. Touched even fleetingly by "a thing of beauty" one can be lifted above common routines and petty afflictions. One's spirits can be sustained long after the transcendent moment. We have the power to affect our surroundings; but our surroundings also have the power to affect us.

The seventeenth-century Dutch, masters of domesticity, capitalized on their surroundings to delight and instruct their young. They commonly set beautiful delft tiles, painted with scenes of children at play, in kitchen baseboards at the eye level of crawling toddlers. The Swedes traditionally have painted walls and lintels with charming designs and words of instruction.

Beautiful surroundings affect inhabitants with implicit as well as explicit messages. "I am what is around me," wrote Wallace Stevens in his poem "Theory"; he added, "Women understand this."[9] Ruth Merton, mother of Trappist monk Thomas Merton, expressed this understanding in a letter to her art instructor: " . . . it seems to me there is no more fascinating subject in the world than the influence of surroundings on human character. And to study character with a view to making its surroundings what they should be by means of certain decoration in houses—that is what I want to try to do."[10]

English-born publishing magnate George Booth founded Cranbrook Academy of Art in the belief that "when sensitiveness to beauty is grafted into minds that are still young and receptive, the result is bound to be most effective."[11]

The powerful influence of beauty was vividly experienced in a most unexpected way by Bill and Peggy Mann. Young and idealistic, they fulfilled their dream of living in New York City on a limited budget by purchasing a run-down brownstone in a run-down neighborhood—West Ninety-fourth Street. Their intentions to become involved in the community and repair the house were constantly foiled. Residents resisted their overtures of friendship, and destructive neighborhood gangs continually sabotaged their long hours of fix-up work. Clearly, they were not welcome.

Almost defeated, they made one more effort to beautify their surroundings. Purchasing materials to construct window boxes, Bill set to work. As some of the trouble-making ringleaders stood on the sidelines eyeing the flats of geraniums and English ivy, an idea occurred to Bill. He offered to give them the material to make their own flower boxes, and he was totally unprepared for their response. With Bill they constructed boxes for their own houses, and other neighborhood children quickly appeared, asking if they too could build a flower box. Soon the windows of West Ninety-fourth Street were lined with flower boxes. Then slowly the miracle took place: Residents started picking up empty beer cans and removing overflowing garbage pails; torn curtains were replaced in windows above the flower boxes. The "Street of Flower Boxes" was transformed not only in appearance but in spirit!

There's an interesting postscript to the story. As the result of a *New York Times* article, a television documentary was eventually made, "The Miracle on West Ninety-fourth Street." But the neighborhood had improved so much that the film was shot on a different street. After the filming was completed, the crew left the flower boxes in the windows. Once again the miracle took place: Inspired by the beauty at their windows, the occupants began to take pride in their surroundings, maintaining their properties and refurbishing their brownstones.

Surely this understanding of human nature was behind the apostle Paul's challenge: "Whatever is true, whatever is noble, whatever is right, whatever is pure, whatever is lovely, whatever is admirable—if anything is excellent or praiseworthy—think about such things" (Phil. 4:8). Whatever elevates our sights above our daily demands serves a good and noble purpose, be it music, a fine line of poetry, a painting, the color scheme of a room, a piece of hand-painted china, or any wonder of God's created order. Work must go on, but there is no need to be bound in spirit to our common tasks.

On the windowsill above my kitchen sink is a tiny pewter girl bending over a purple crocus. Above the scene of much of my labor, it is a gentle reminder of Paul's instruction: If anything is excellent or praiseworthy, think on these things. I cannot eliminate the trivial, repetitive, or annoying aspects of my daily life, but I can surround myself and my family with beauty. I can turn from that which binds my spirit to the true, noble, pure, and lovely that liberates.

# CHAPTER 4

## YOUR STORY

1. What did Wallace Stevens mean when he wrote, "I am what is around me"? In what ways are you influenced by your domestic surroundings?
2. How do you think your children and spouse are affected by their surroundings? How did your childhood domestic environment affect you?
3. What elements of beauty currently bring joy into your life?
4. In what additional ways could you realistically bring beauty into your home?

# A TIME TO GROW
## ELEMENTS OF STYLE
## ARE MODIFIED BY SITUATION

"It's my ball!" shouts Jonathan.

From the morning room I watch him kick the brick edging of my flower garden, trample through the plants, and scoop up the basketball. He leaps for a jump shot and lands with both feet on top of my largest Gerber daisy. Oblivious to the injury inflicted on the bed of Gerbers, he dashes back through the garden to retrieve the ball from David who waits expectantly under the hoop.

I survey the damages. One brick is dislodged from the border. A path is crushed from one end of the foliage to the other; several blooms have been snapped off their stems.

But in all fairness to Jonathan, the garden does not exactly command respect. Large patches of earth are exposed near the hoop end of the flower bed. Weeds are almost indistinguishable from the remaining foliage. Other blooms are hanging from broken stems; some have gone to seed.

The Gerber garden has seen better days. I remember marking out two triangular plots on either side of the backyard walk. I tilled the soil, enriched it with peat, and bordered it with bricks. I set out healthy green plants in rows, packing rich soil around them, taking great care not to cover their crowns. Then daily, sometimes twice a day, I watered the thirsty plants, delighting to see any drooping blooms turn their heads once again to the sun.

It wasn't long until the plants were producing a continuous show of blooms. Heady with this success, I began to fill in spaces with more plants until my garden was a sea of green bobbing with blossoms of pink and red, coral and yellow. Year around I picked blossoms for centerpieces, gracing shelves and tables with little containers of colorful daisies.

My reputation spread. Friends asked if I wouldn't spare some blooms for them to use in lunch bouquets. They asked for gardening advice. Modestly I explained that it was all in the site and the soil. "Of course you must faithfully water them," I would add. Little matter that gardening manuals ranked Gerbers "easy to grow"! I was the unchallenged Gerber queen of Lake Wales. It was glorious.

But it didn't last. You see the "right site" for the garden was also the perfect place for children to play. At first I would keep vigilant guard over my floral kingdom. From the morning room I would bang on the window when a ball or a boy would invade my territory. From an open window I would plead, command, or threaten, "One more ball in the garden and you'll have to play across the street!" Invariably I was forced to leave my throne and banish the boys from the backyard. And a changing of the guard was unsatisfactory: "The children are in the garden again," I'd admonish my husband, who was supposed to be doing duty from his morning room chair.

It's hard to sustain a one-person defense: me against the world. It became easier to ignore these assaults than to face the foe. Not that it was total surrender. Occasionally I continued to pull weeds, drench a flower bed, bark a threat from the window. But the battle reports were irreversible. Bare patches advanced; greenery retreated.

Yes, I laid down my arms, but I still have my dreams. Someday I'll have a cottage garden outside my kitchen door. A profusion of flowers of assorted sizes, shapes, and colors will spill over walks and borders. (I won't limit myself to Gerbers. *Anyone* can grow Gerbers!) The lawn will be outlined with thick green hedges and bordered with rich beds of soil for cutting gardens. And I'll have a rose garden with dozens of bushes in shades of pink and coral. In the center I'll place a statuary or perhaps a bird bath. Maybe I'll sow some wildflower seeds—have a field of wildflowers! Then I'll stake a garden motto discreetly amidst my blooms:

> The kiss of the sun for pardon
> The song of a bird for mirth.
> One's nearer God's heart in the garden
> Than anywhere else on earth.

*Someday.* But for now I'll content myself with window boxes, hanging plants, clay pots—and a backyard of happy children. "There is a time for everything, and a season for every activity under heaven" (Eccl. 3:1). I can always cultivate a garden. But, for me, *now* is the time to cultivate children.

## YOUR STORY

1. How does the presence of children affect your decorating schemes? To what extent do you "childproof" your home? At what point should children be required to respect their surroundings?

2. Make a point of observing your performance in the home. How much of your energy and effort is directed toward the protection of things?
3. What plans do you have for your home—after the children are grown? Is the presence of loved ones adequate compensation to you for certain material adjustments?

# MY FAVORITE THINGS
# ELEMENTS OF STYLE ARE IMBUED WITH INTANGIBLE SIGNIFICANCE

Cherished things possess an intangible magic. Objects, through past association or meaningful connotation, form a personal and private world around us. They can recall special places, people, and experiences. They can also evoke dreams and aspirations beyond our immediate reach. Personal possessions can create a time-defying sense of permanency, bringing a familiar world to foreign places. They even can serve to transport us to exotic lands.

The objects I've accumulated over the years have more emotional appeal than actual value. The criterion for selection is simple: They are loved. I've documented summer vacations with objects collected on site—seashells from Key Biscayne, stones gathered on a cross-country trip to California, a pair of Staffordshire teapots bought on Cape Cod, a rose-sprigged biscuit basket from the Midwest. Framed prints of gardens and selected postcards of castles and cathedrals reveal dreams of future trips. I display anticipations of leisurely moments in china teacups and linen napkins. I store noble intentions in pretty boxes of unused stationery.

When, exactly, does an accumulation of things become a collection? It's hard to say. "Like love, it just happens,"[12] suggested Dee Hardie. Beginning in early childhood, my mother gave me heart-shaped boxes to celebrate my "almost-Valentine's Day" birthday. Later I became a collector of hearts *and* boxes! Boxes never cease to fascinate me: dainty porcelain boxes with delicate designs, lidded boxes of any shape or size in which to hide treasures or, like Winnie the Pooh, to "store useful things."

My fascination with domestic dwellings led to my collection of little houses. How can I resist a tiny wooden alpine chalet, a stone Cotswold cottage, a stucco Spanish villa, a row of Dutch canal houses, a clay pagoda, or a well-crafted bird's nest?

I don't remember when the first angel flew into my life, but at present a host of angels inhabit the morning room. One of terra-cotta keeps vigil from the top shelf of the bookcase; a papier-mâché angel hovers from a floor lamp to keep watch over my reading. A beatific brass cherub poses from his pedestal on the desk next to an impish sprite carrying a slingshot on his back—a remarkable resemblance to Jonathan! A Florentine print of Gabriel rules the heavenly host from a gold-gilt Gothic frame—a gift from an octogenarian, his own wedding gift.

Memorabilia scattered throughout the house in picture frames, on tables and walls, serve as a visual history of the family. A brass teapot, a silk watercolor, a pair of cloisonné planters—all recall Dave's childhood in China. Twenty Indiana summers are captured in wicker furniture and a banjo clock that laboriously grinds out the hours. A half-dozen montages categorize our sentimental clutter. Framed paintings plus colorful pottery and papier-mâché document various stages of the children's lives.

Among our most treasured things are the thoughtfully selected gifts from friends. Then there are the bibelots—

objects of curiosity, beauty, or rarity. Displayed singularly or grouped in little still lifes, they provide a continual source of visual delight.

Often certain objects carry significance far beyond appearance—icons of a sort, material representations of spiritual truths. Two Danish medallions, "Day" and "Night"—exquisite angels in porcelain relief—quicken my spirit with their beauty and their comforting reminder of divine protection: "For he will command his angels concerning you to guard you in all your ways" (Ps. 91:11).

Accessories not only please the dweller but give home its heart and feeling. "People remember houses in terms of details and touches," observed Dorothy Rodgers in *My Favorite Things*. "The pleasure you find in objects you care for lends them a special quality that others sense and share."[13] In my memory the gracious dwelling of an elderly woman will forever be associated with the heady scent of jasmine. The dining room of one young homemaker is distinguished by a silk cherry-colored kimono stretched on one wall, setting the color scheme and an oriental theme for the entire room. Artifacts from around the world create a memorable ambience in another friend's home. " . . . An heirloom chest, a porcelain box, a big bowl of peonies, though not artistically remarkable or expensive—are infinitely more effective in creating atmosphere than an acre of costly neutral carpet," continues Dorothy Rodgers. "The latter is there of necessity; the chest, the procelain, the flowers are there because you love them."[14]

Sometimes I wonder if I should simplify my cluttered life, pare down the objects. It would be practical and sensible: minimize housekeeping, clarify my existence. But I can't. Not now. Objects speak to me. They tell of people and places I love, of experiences and events I want to savor.

# CHAPTER 4

They beckon of places to visit and things to do—someday.
It's the favorite things, priceless because they mean something, that make our home lovely—and truly ours.

## YOUR STORY

1. What were your favorite objects in your childhood
   home?
2. If you could keep only three objects from your present
   home, what would they be? Why?
3. What objects or collections in your home are most
   representative of you? Why? What objects are most
   representative of other family members?

# ALL GOOD GIFTS
# ELEMENTS OF STYLE ARE GRANTED
# TEMPORAL STATUS

*All good gifts around us*
*Are sent from heaven above;*
*Then thank the Lord,*
*O thank the Lord*
*For all His love.*
                    —*Matthias Claudius*

How lovely the house looks today! Invigorated by the brisk, breezy weather, this morning I opened the windows and tackled the long-delayed tasks of waxing and polishing. Now the house shines from my industry. I've rubbed dull wooden surfaces to a soft luster and polished silver and brass to a glow.

Consider the Hepplewhite breakfront, stately and tall against the dining room wall. Normally I would be satisfied with a quick, cursory dusting. Not today. Removing objects cluttering the surface, I rubbed creamy wax into the mahogany wood with a soft cotton cloth. Slowly the fine-grained wood took on a new radiance. Its delicate strips of inlay stood out in amber relief. Opening the butler's drawer, I wiped an accumulation of dust from little pigeonholes that display tiny treasures. With the greatest of care I polished panes of glass between the wooden fretwork on the cabinet doors that guard our china.

This inanimate piece of furniture seems to take on a new reality in response to my loving caress. It becomes a vital presence with which to reckon. Where has it been, what has it seen in the centuries of its existence? From what forest were trees felled? Who designed its cabinets, drawers, and

145

cubbyholes? Who set the inlay into the façade and finished the mahoghany? What conversations has it overheard? What celebrations has it witnessed?

Loving maintenance rejuvenates everyday objects, giving them greater beauty and a heightened level of intimacy. "The housewife awakens furniture that was asleep," maintained Gaston Bachelard. "A house that shines from the care that it receives appears to have been rebuilt from the inside; it is as though it were new inside."[15]

The house does shine from my special attentions. I exalt in its sparkling cleanness and unaccustomed order. I know it won't be long before fingerprints smudge sparkling windows. Books and magazines will soon clutter surfaces. It's just a matter of time before dust will gather and metals tarnish. But for now I glory in its perfection. I love this place that ministers to my spirit as it serves the practical needs of our family.

Do I love my home too much? Can a place be too dear to one's heart? I was first faced with this question when preparing to move into it. I remember walking through its empty rooms waiting for new occupants. How I savored the character of the spacious old house with its enrichments of wood moldings and lintels, brass doorknobs and wall sconces, French doors and fireplaces. The floors had been sanded and stained a dark walnut finish. Walls were freshly painted in colors that captured the desired mood of each room. Looking out the window to our snug little "Best Nest" across the street, I felt like an adulterous wife forsaking her faithful husband for a dashing lover. I loved this house! It had all I had ever yearned for in a home but never dreamed of having.

When we finally moved, the reality of the house, unlike most dreams, exceeded my expectations. From the first evening it looked and *felt* like home. Even the children sensed this. Earlier, traditionalist David had consoled his brother, "It's okay, Jonathan. I know the new place is not as nice as ours, but you'll get used to it." A week later when asked, "Does it seem as much like home to you as our other house?" David replied, "*More* like home."

I think I know what he meant. We had to work to make the other house "work" for us, to overcome limitations of size, layout, and location. This house almost begged to be lived in.

Ironically the luxury of moving into the larger manse did present some problems for me. I discovered that one could live with limitations more easily than with luxury. As I struggled to reconcile this undeserved bounty, a portion of a letter from Bonhoeffer's *Letters and Papers from Prison* spoke directly to my heart:

> We ought to find and love God in what He actually gives us; if it pleases Him to allow us to enjoy some overwhelming earthly happiness, we mustn't try to be more pious than God Himself and allow happiness to be corrupted by presumption and arrogance, and by unbridled religious fantasy which is never satisfied with what God gives. God will see to it that the man who finds Him in his earthly happiness and thanks Him for it does not lack reminder that earthly things are transient, that it is good for him to attune his heart to what is eternal, and that sooner or later there will be times when he can say in all sincerity, "I wish I were home." But everything has its time, and the main thing is that we keep in step with God.[16]

For me the application was immediate and profound. There was no merit in rejecting any good gift from God, in my case, this home. Rather than be so presumptuous as to challenge God's provision, I should enjoy it for this moment, always remembering where it fits into the eternal scheme: temporal, transitory. The test as to whether or not I maintain that perspective is whether or not I can release it, should that time come—but not before.

*Do* I love my home too much? What is its claim on my life? Is it a gift from God for whatever time or purpose He wills? Could I leave it for a lesser place? In short, does it own me?

The test is in the daily living. Is it a place for people or a museum for things? Am I enslaved by housekeeping? What happens when the first fingerprint smudges my breakfront's spotless windows, when clean surfaces are strewn with clutter? How much of my time, money, and energy is invested in maintaining this place? Is it used for my purposes or for God's? The ultimate test will be in leaving. If called could I say, "Here am I Lord. Send me"?

Do I love my home too much? The answer comes not one time but each time I am tested. It comes daily in my choices. It comes periodically in my responses to specific challenges to release something precious. It comes in a spirit of gratitude that can praise God in any place for all the good gifts He sends.

*Thank You for this home, dear Father. Thank You for its loveliness and for its loving embrace of family and friends. May I enjoy it as You would have me enjoy any earthly pleasure, remembering always that it is not my final destination but merely an inn along my pilgrim-way home. Amen.*

## YOUR STORY

1. What does your present home mean to you?
2. To what extent does your house affect your major decisions? Would you be willing to leave it for another place? Would you be content to remain in it?
3. How much does home maintenance dominate your life? How much time, energy, or money do you devote to its upkeep?
4. Do you perceive your home as an inn or as your final destination?

# CHAPTER 5
# DOORS AND THRESHOLDS:
# THE OPEN DOOR OF HOSPITALITY

*An architect designs doors to permit proper access to the house. On the threshold of hospitality, a homemaker opens those doors to embrace outsiders.*

# THE GLORY OF THE HOUSE IS HOSPITALITY

*Hospitality involves many aspects of giving and receiving in relation to friends, acquaintances, and strangers.*

"May I help?" Kimberly offers, crowding me at the sink, the anchor point from which I pivot to stove and refrigerator in my final preparation for company dinner.

"Oh, Kimberly," I sigh, having difficulty managing myself under pressure, much less eager and inexperienced volunteer help.

"Do you want me to put sherbet in the glasses?" she presses.

"Well . . . okay. But be careful not to drop any on the tray."

Why do the children invariably position themselves in the thick of activity? Jonathan has been in and out of the kitchen with an endless stream of comments and questions. David has chosen the moment of countdown to lean against the kitchen counter and detail the events of his day. Even Kimberly's offer of help seems yet one more element to factor into the great final effort.

I flash back in time to another kitchen some thirty years ago. The aroma of pot roast fills the house. Gravy simmers on the stove top. Mother rushes from stove to countertop, checking the rolls, stirring the gravy. Wisps of hair escape the figure-eight chignon clinging to the nape of her moist

CHAPTER 5

neck. She removes a round china tray from a fitted cardboard box and sets it on the kitchen table.

"May I help?" I offer eagerly as she begins arranging carrot curls and radish flowers in the divided compartments.

"Not just now. Go see if the cracker dish needs refilling," she suggests, handing me a Nabisco box.

"May I have some?" I persist.

"Just one," she sighs, rushing to rescue the rolls from the oven.

Off I skip through the dining room to retrieve the empty bowl. The table is set in festive finery for company fare. In the living room, guests sip pineapple shrubs while Father regales them with time-tested tales. The house is alive with sounds of laughter and aromas of scrumptious food. My heart bursts with joy.

"The glory of the house is hospitality," reads the hand-stitched sampler. Even a child can sense it. Hosts are expansive; guests are grateful. For house and host alike, the arrival of a guest is a glorious moment empowered by the special philosophy of hospitality: "A guest is someone who's done you an honor by visiting—so it's your duty to do everything in your power to make him feel welcome."[1]

Most cultures place a high value on hospitality, some elevating it almost to the divine. The Polish have a saying, "Guest at home is equal to God at home." The ancient Greeks were encouraged to be hospitable by a tradition that held that Zeus might appear in the guise of a stranger. The Chinese, mindful of a history of hunger, have traditionally equated hospitality with food and, in turn, with life. Once they have shared food with another, they consider them-selves bound as friends.

"A golden thread running through the stories of the household of faith is the theme of hospitality,"[2] wrote Edith

154

# THE GLORY OF THE HOUSE IS HOSPITALITY

Deen in *Family Living in the Bible*. The children of Israel were instructed to love the stranger, "because you were aliens in Egypt" (Exod. 23:9). The prophet Isaiah defined true fasting, in part: "to share your food with the hungry and to provide the poor wanderer with shelter" (Isa. 58:7). Christ promised that we will be blessed when we invite "the poor, the crippled, the lame, the blind" (Luke 14:13) to our houses to eat with us. Paul insisted that church leaders "be . . . hospitable" (1 Tim. 3:2), and Peter charged first-century Christians to "offer hospitality to one another" (1 Peter 4:9).

What then is hospitality? The German word for hospitality, *gastfreundschaft,* means friendship for the guest. Henri Nouwen has noted that the Dutch word, *gastorijheid,* means freedom of the guest, implying that hospitality is "friendship without binding the guest and freedom without leaving him alone."[3] Karen Mains has observed, "Ultimately, this is what we offer when we open our home in the true spirit of hospitality. We offer shelter. We offer healing."[4] True hospitality is love in action. It is opening our hearts to our guests as we open the door of our homes.

The front door of our house, as with our former homes, is painted a welcoming red. A visiting Episcopalian priest, noting the color, observed that in medieval times a red door connoted a place of sanctuary. Since then I have adopted this apt symbolism. I like to believe our red door signifies sanctuary. When it swings open, all visitors— friends and strangers—may step over the threshold into the loving safety of our home and hearts.

O God, make the door of the house wide enough
to receive all who need human love and fellowship, narrow enough to shut out all envy, pride,

# CHAPTER 5

and strife. Make its threshold smooth enough to be no stumbling-block to children, nor to straying feet, but rugged and strong enough to turn back the tempter's power. God, make the door of this house the gateway to Thine eternal kingdom —Inscription above door of Saint Stephen's in London.

## YOUR STORY

1. What was the role of hospitality in your childhood home?
2. Why do you think hospitality is given such high value in most cultures?
3. What is the biblical rationale for hospitality?
4. How do you define *hospitality*?

# A SHELTERING HOOD
# HOSPITALITY IS LOVE IN ACTION

*I remember a house where all*
*  were good*
*To me, God knows, deserving*
*  no such thing:*
*Comforting smell breathed at*
*  very entering,*
*Fetched fresh, as I suppose,*
*  off some sweet wood.*
*That cordial air made those*
*  kind people a hood*
*All over, as a bevy of eggs*
*  the mothering wing*
*Will, or mild nights the new*
*  morsels of Spring.*
*            —Gerard Manley Hopkins*

Shrieks of laughter outside my window awaken me from a late afternoon nap. Amidst the sounds of mallets cracking against croquet balls, the children and their grandfather argue specific shots and discuss fine points of the game. The scent of newly mown grass awakens memories of past summers. Filtered light from the afternoon sun illuminates this little corner room I occupied throughout my youth. I study the pink room lovingly readied for our occupancy— the white painted furniture, the rose fabric-covered chair, groupings of family pictures over the desk and bed. In the distance I hear the clink of ice cubes as Mother pours water into glass tumblers. A familiar aroma wafting from the

CHAPTER 5

kitchen suggests that our evening meal will be Mother's famous meat loaf accompanied, no doubt, by baked potatoes and acorn squash oozing with buttery brown sugar sprinkled with nutmeg. Gratitude wells up within me as I once again enjoy the "cordial air," the "comforting smells" of my parents' home, the place of my earliest experience of hospitality.

Since leaving my parents' home, others have spread over me the sheltering hood of hospitality. My most vivid memories of hospitality are those forged during times of greatest need, including my first year away from home as a college student. By the good fortune of a new friendship, I was included in a Bible study group led by the college president's wife. I don't recall what we studied. I've forgotten who else attended. I do remember leaving my hectic campus existence and entering her warm and welcoming home. That one hour, late Tuesday afternoons, was a "hood all over" to me, a bewildered freshman struggling to manage my new independence.

Dave's fieldwork during his seminary years was some sixty miles from our apartment. Often on Fridays or Saturdays, at the end of a hard week of study and teaching, we'd head off to a youth group function, returning on Sunday. One church couple, themselves struggling with financial setbacks, offered us the use of their unfinished garage apartment. "It's not much, but you're welcome to spend nights there or escape to it during the day." Not only did they open their apartment to us; they shared with us their family meals. The busy seminary years were immeasurably enriched by "these kind people" who gave us what we sorely needed—a place to relax and sleep, the fellowship of a family.

Several weeks after the birth of Jonathan, while I was

homebound with three young children, the phone rang with
the irresistible invitation: "When Dave comes home at noon,
leave the baby and children with him, and I'll pick you up
for lunch. Come in your robe if you wish; we're eating at
my house." I'll never forget the welcome of this unexpected
respite. My hostess led me into the family room where a
fragrant evergreen was decorated for Christmas. She pulled
a tea cart set for lunch up to the hearth, where a fire crackled
and glowed. Christmas carols played in the background. I
spooned creamy tomato soup topped with whipping cream
into my mouth and feasted on velvety quiche. I enjoyed
adult conversation over a cup of hot spiced tea, relishing the
peace and calm of this oasis in my baby-regulated schedule.
"Comforting smell breathed at very entering, Fetched fresh,
as I suppose, off some sweet wood."

We returned to Illinois for our twentieth reunion from
high school during a particularly stressful time in ministry.
The mother of a former classmate insisted we stay with her.
"Don't worry about a thing. There's plenty of room for all
of us!" We moved in, five-strong, and she demonstrated her
special brand of hospitality. Each morning a freshly brewed
pot of coffee greeted us upon entering the kitchen. A variety
of child-pleasing cereal boxes lined the countertop. Clothing
placed in the washing machine emerged, miraculously, dry
and folded! Our hostess was mysteriously absent when old
classmates gathered and comfortably present when we were
eager to reminisce about old times or discuss current
problems—a "mothering wing" over a "bevy of eggs."

Words cannot convey how the sheltering hood of
hospitality has ministered to our family through the years:
the open door of a friend's home . . . conversation over a
cup of coffee . . . a safe place to deposit a child temporarily
. . . a shoulder to cry on . . . a listening ear . . . a quiet home

in which to listen to music or to converse . . . a space to be alone . . . a home-cooked holiday meal . . . a dinner at a fine restaurant. Hospitality has many forms and functions from the simple delights of casual acquaintance to the radical ministry of deep friendship. But always it is a "mothering wing"—a sheltering hood.

Ah, yes, I remember, I remember a house where all was good to me. I remember *many* houses where all was good to me, "God knows, deserving no such thing."

## YOUR STORY

1. When has hospitality been a "sheltering hood" for you?
2. What elements made those experiences special?

# A PORTION OF ONESELF
# HOSPITALITY IS A GIFT TO OTHERS

"The only gift is a portion of thyself," wrote Ralph Waldo Emerson, offering in one phrase the secret of giving and the key to hospitality. As obvious as it seems when stated, it took years for me to grow truly comfortable with this simple understanding of hospitality. At the heart of my misconception, I suspect, was my unchallenged effort to pick up where my mother left off. Without considering her years of experience or our different personalities and life-styles, I knocked myself out to entertain "mother-style."

One incident early in my marriage demonstrates this error and provided me with a "moment of truth." I had invited friends to our apartment for dinner. With memories of candlelight dinners at their home, I foraged through my cooking primers for recipes worthy of such honored guests. I brought our china out of storage and polished seldom-used silverware.

The day of the event, I raced home from school and much like a whirling dervish flew into an all-out effort to put the house in company order and attend to my culinary preparations. Operating on the principle that "all's well that ends well," I intended to duplicate an exotic dessert featured in a current periodical: a honeydew melon carved into petals, filled with frosted grapes, and studded with fresh daisies. Propping up the magazine, I set to work. Slicing the top off the melon, I removed the seeds and began the almost impossible task of carving symmetrical petals from the top down into the base. Desperately working against the clock, I rinsed the grapes and tried to master the frosting procedure. As I was rinsing a handful of daisies, Dave cheerfully announced, "They're here!" I restrained an impulse to toss the daisies in his face!

Given the circumstances, the dinner went amazingly well. In a suppressed state of tension I served the appetizers. Then I began to relax during the main course. By dessert time I was feeling downright expansive and eager to present the sculptured wonder! Arranging my creation on a pedestal dish, I carried it into the living room and placed it on the table. After a moment of astonished silence, my dinner companions burst into gales of laughter. (None, I noted, laughed harder than Dave!) The hilarity continued as Dave performed the technically difficult feat of carving individual slices from the extraordinary bloom. Frosted grapes scattered across the table. When a curious insect emerged from the petal of one pristine daisy, we all split our sides.

After the guests left (still chuckling as they walked down the driveway), I asked Dave, "Why was the dessert so funny?"

Grinning Dave answered, "I think it started with the look on your face when you came out with that pedestal dish." More seriously he added, "I guess it just wasn't *you*."

Sheepishly I reconsidered my endeavors to entertain. At the end of a week of teaching, I had neither the time nor the energy to serve a full-course dinner—much less one topped by a complicated dessert! However well-meaning, my elaborate efforts had almost been my undoing. Fortunately for all, the absurdity of the dessert provided the comic relief that saved the evening.

The heart of hospitality is the gift of oneself. It is the offering of one's heart and home—with all the strengths and limitations of one's immediate life situation. More important than what one serves or the condition of the house is what one offers of oneself to the guests. Karen Mains has maintained that "*entertaining* has little to do with real hospitality. Secular entertainment is a terrible bondage. Its source is human pride. Demanding perfection, fostering the urge to impress, it is a rigorous taskmaster which enslaves. In contrast, Scriptural hospitality is a freedom which liberates."[5]

This liberation was joyously demonstrated by one veteran in true hospitality. The day after moving into a new apartment, Maud called, inviting us to join several friends for dinner to celebrate her husband's seventy-first birthday. Amongst packing crates and boxes, pictures propped against walls, we ate a five-course Belgian supper on a table spread with linen, china, and silver service. A more festive occasion could not be imagined. Little did we know that a terminal illness would soon limit future celebrations. What if she had waited to celebrate until the house was "ready"?

In my heart alongside this gala affair rank memories of other occasions when friends opened their homes—just as they were—and invited us in: the young mother with four children who served me hot chocolate while she folded her laundry on the dining room table; the couple who roasted hot dogs with us in the fireplace of their unfurnished living room; the family who brought us home after church during a snowstorm and salvaged leftovers from their refrigerator while I washed the breakfast dishes; the bachelor who offers us the quiet retreat of his lakeshore home in which to

163

converse and listen to music; the widow who keeps a fresh supply of goodies and the open invitation to "stop in anytime." On and on goes the list of people who have enriched our lives by simply offering *themselves*.

True hospitality requires only that we open our homes and offer our personal resources—be they great or small. It is irrelevant whether we impulsively invite people in for coffee and Sara Lee cake after a game or concert or plan weeks in advance for a formal sit-down dinner. Little matter whether we serve from paper plates and cups or from fine china. What matters is that hospitality be a heartfelt expression appropriate to our personalities and our life situations.

Along with the comfort implicit in this understanding of hospitality is a challenge. If what I'm offering is "a gift of myself," then the question must follow: What kind of a person am I? Am I a sensitive hostess? Do I listen for the spoken—or unspoken—messages of my guests? Am I really listening or am I waiting my turn to speak? Am I aware of the needs or uncertainties of my guests? Is their comfort and welfare my greatest concern? Henri Nouwen has claimed that "Poverty makes a good host," explaining that "poverty of mind" is freedom from an overabundance of ideas, opinions, and corrections; "poverty of heart" is freedom from prejudice, worry, and self.[6]

A story about Queen Victoria captures for me the essence of hospitality. A formal dinner was given to honor a commoner who had distinguished himself in service to his country. Clearly out of his league at this auspicious occasion, the nervous guest dropped a crystal goblet, which shattered upon the stone floor. Shocked to silence, the company awaited the queen's response, knowing full well the shattered vessel was from her prize collection of heirloom crystal. Without so much as a moment's hesitation, the queen smiled at her horrified guest and said reassuringly, "Don't worry. I have many more." Then to emphasize her point, she reached for her own goblet and dropped it to the floor. As recklessly lavish as that gesture may seem, it demonstrated in no uncertain terms the value she placed on the comfort of her guests.

Through the years I continue to struggle to balance my dreams and desire to be hospitable with the reality of my changing life situation. When my children were young, it was easier to have guests in for dessert after the children were in bed. Now, with the children's assistance and added years of experience, I can do what once would have defeated me. (Who knows? Maybe I'll pull out the old honeydew, grapes, and daisies routine one of these days!) Little matter: Regardless of substance and style, the essence of hospitality is the gift of oneself.

## YOUR STORY

1. In what respect should hospitality be a "gift of oneself"?
2. How do you distinguish hospitality from entertainment?
3. What is your personal ideal of hospitality? What has shaped this idea? How realistic is it in light of your present situation?
4. In what ways could you now open the door of your home in hospitality?

# COMPANY'S COMING!
# HOSPITALITY IS A PRIVILEGE

"Kimberly, you're going to have to move your things out of your room right now. Our company will be here in less than an hour!"

Shifting into high gear, I enter the last stretch of my preparations for overnight guests. I can feel the tension build as I attend to the final details: Place clean towels in the bathroom; add fresh bars of soap; put a rocking chair into our makeshift "guest room"; plump the pillows in the living room. As I work, I review mentally my checklist of things to do before our guests' arrival (my guarantee of enjoying the occasion): house in order; groceries purchased; table set for supper; children instructed in rerouting of bathing and sleeping procedures. How I'd love to prepare a guest room with thoughtful amenities: desk stocked with writing paper and matching envelopes; padded hangers in the closet; fresh flowers on the dresser; a bowl of fruit . . . Next time.

Amidst my inevitable rushed and hectic last-minute preparations, I have no reservations. I'm committed. Underlying the work, stress, and momentary inconvenience of hosting is the privilege of having company. At the start, the very act of opening the door of hospitality presupposes bounty. A roof to shelter, food to share, fellowship to offer are but tangible evidences of one's being blessed.

I first learned this truth on a choir trip when I was in high school. Carefully instructed by our leaders that "service" did not end with the concert but extended into the homes that hosted us, my roommate and I were nonetheless taken aback by the shabby and crowded dwelling to which we were assigned one night. Even the warmth of the hot chocolate served by our elderly hostess could not remove the chill of the Canadian evening from this unheated apartment. Weary from days of travel and evenings of singing, we had to stifle yawns as our hostess produced pictures and tales of her geographically scattered family.

With relief we sank at last into the double bed that filled the tiny room separated from the kitchen by only a curtain. I lay in bed listening to our hostess wash the cups and saucers, straighten the chairs around the table. Finally the lights were switched off. The only sound was the ticking of a clock. Slipping out of bed to visit the bathroom, I groped my way into the kitchen and stumbled into a large object. I adjusted my focus to the moonlit room. Sound asleep in a straight chair was our hostess, a blanket wrapped around her street clothes! Totally absorbed in the discomfort of our "unlucky draw," it hadn't occurred to me to wonder where *she* was sleeping. "Jean," I whispered, returning to our room, "we have *her* room. She's sitting up all night!"

Early the next morning we woke to the wonderful aromas of sizzling bacon and English muffins toasting on an oven rack. Two humbled girls sat at the kitchen table trying now to give of ourselves in some small way to one who had given us her rare gift—all that she had.

I recall reading about an image that Elisabeth Elliot remembered from her childhood: For her the privilege of

167

sharing one's resources—whatever they may be—was represented in a jar kept on the fireplace mantel. Here during financially strapped depression years, the family placed money to be shared with others in need. It never occurred to her that her family was poor. As long as they had something to give to others, she assumed they were well off.

Blessings received in exchange for hospitality underscore the fundamental biblical principle stressed in the Prayer of Saint Francis: "It is in giving that we receive." Our family has repeatedly experienced returns in excess for any sacrifice of time, energy, money, or wear and tear involved in hospitality. The children recall with delight the evening we hosted a Pakistanian gentleman, moderator of his national church. As Dave and I extended ourselves in an all-out effort to bridge a perceived language barrier, the children valiantly tried to suppress their amusement. Speaking slowly—and loudly—we pointed and gestured to convey the simplest messages: "Would you like some coffee?" (great sweeping arm motion, sipping from an imaginary cup); "What kind of animals do you have in Pakistan?" (barking, meowing, general barnyard noises). Pointing at the piano, the harp, a ball on the floor, I shouted in clearly enunciated syllables: "Do You Have An-y Hob-bies?" "Yes," he responded in perfect English, "archaeology." He went on to develop at length in fluent English the historical treasures of his country and his concern that they were being depleted by other wealthier countries!

We—both children and parents—were rewarded when we broke the feigned language barrier by penetrating the real cultural barrier. We enjoyed the remaining evening and following day with our entertaining guest who catered to Kimberly ("Daughters are the flowers in the garden of family") and provided the transcultural experience of singing native hymns while accompanying himself on the piano.

Potentially, hospitality brings benefits to all involved. Henri Nouwen claimed, "Guest and host alike can reveal their most precious gifts and bring new life to each other."[7] Surely our children's horizons have been stretched beyond the limits of our social, cultural, and racial backgrounds through guests in our home. They have lingered at the table to hear elderly friends recall tales of "when I was young." They have been entertained by anecdotes and skits of visiting speakers unwinding from public ministry. They have been inspired by impromptu performances of guest recitalists. They have been challenged to respond to the needs of hurting and needy people. In short, through hospitality our children have benefited from experiences broader than what one family can provide.

By necessity our children have always been involved in the hospitality of this home, as they have had to shift their schedules, share their spaces, and provide services to accommodate guests. Now we actively employ their assistance, articulating their contributions so they can consciously participate in the blessings.

Recently Kimberly received a thank-you note from a minister who had occupied her room during a conference at our church:

> Dear Kimberly,
>
> Just a note to thank you for giving up your room to me. I know that is not always easy. But you did that very gracefully. God tells us to give up what is one's and then He will give back even more. I think you have learned that lesson.

169

CHAPTER 5

A big brother in the Lord,
Brother Tat

His letter succinctly summarized for Kimberly the privilege of hospitality. Likewise, it holds important truth for us all.

## YOUR STORY

1. What are your happiest recollections of friends in your home? What made these experiences pleasurable?
2. What does Henri Nouwen mean when he states, "Guest and host alike can bring new life to each other"?
3. Is your home a welcoming refuge for your friends? If not, what factors prevent this form of hospitality?

# THE PLEASURE OF THEIR COMPANY
## HOSPITALITY INCLUDES OUR CHILDREN

"Okay. Today we are going to get to the bottom of this," I say, pointing out the black scuff marks scarring the kitchen floor.

"It's not *me!*" chorus the children from the kitchen table.

"It really doesn't matter *who* it is," I explain. "I simply want to know whose shoes are making the marks, so it doesn't happen again."

The children hotly proclaim their innocence.

"Listen. I'm not *blaming* anyone. It's just that yesterday I scrubbed the floor on my hands and knees. Now today the floor is covered with scuff marks. No one else has been here since I scrubbed the floor, so now is a good time to find out whose shoes are leaving the marks."

"They can't be mine, 'cause none of my shoes even have black in them," declares Kimberly.

"Well, they're someone's," I state logically.

"Jonathan," accuses David, pointing at his brother.

"They're not mine," he flashes.

"Even if they are, it's all right," I insist.

"But they're *not* mine," he continues. "I'm wearing tennis shoes."

CHAPTER 5

"You wore your church shoes this morning," I remind him.

"See, you *do* think it's me. You said you were trying to find out who—but you *all* think it's *me*."

"Even if it is you, it's all right," I repeat. "I just want to find out who it is so it doesn't happen again. I spent hours yesterday scrubbing the floors. Now it's worse than when I started. And it's not the first time."

"You all think it's me," Jonathan reports indignantly.

I must admit he is a likely candidate. Observing the pattern of marks, I can almost see him sliding to the sink, rounding the corner to the laundry room, skidding out the back door.

"Why don't we just get his shoes and see?" Kimberly suggests with uncommonly good sense.

"Go get your shoes, Jonathan," needles David.

"It's *not* me," Jonathan mutters as he heads off.

Jonathan returns with his shoes. Dave takes them from him and firmly rubs the edges against the floor. Nothing.

"Do it harder," I command.

Nothing.

"See!" Jonathan exalts. "I told you so. No one would believe me."

"Go get *your* Sunday shoes, David."

"Why? It couldn't be my shoes."

"Just get your shoes. Honestly," I add, "you don't need to be so defensive. No one has done anything wrong. I just want to prevent this from happening again."

David returns with his shoes. Dave repeats the procedure.

Nothing.

"Are you sure you wore those shoes today?" I ask.

"Mom! They're the only shoes that fit!"

172

"Go get your shoes, Kimberly," the boys sing.

"It must be your shoes, Dave," I observe as Kimberly leaves the room. "I don't see how her flats could leave black marks."

Dave and Kimberly return with their shoes. Suspense mounts as Dave scrapes Kimberly's shoes against the floor. Nothing.

"Do yours, Dad," hoot the obviously relieved children.

Dave bends over and scrapes his shoe against the floor. Nothing.

"Do the other side," I tell him.

Nothing.

"Do it harder," I insist.

Nothing.

"Mother?!" David dares to speak my name.

"Go get your shoes, Mother!" the children chime.

The room is charged with drama upon my return.

The children gather around Dave as he bends down to scrape my improbable slipper against the kitchen floor. He begins to shake. Jonathan is on all fours. "It's Mother!" he shrieks.

"Let me see," I demand.

Dave swipes a shoe against the floor. A jet black streak remains. With whoops of laughter the children taunt: "There goes Mother sliding out to the sink! There goes Mother streaking across the kitchen. Now she's rounding the corner." Dave, who is still shaking with mirth, has the good sense to say nothing.

So we've gotten to the bottom of the truth. Didn't I say that's what I wanted? Why, then, do I feel so foolish? This revelation is my moment of truth: For all my talk ("Nobody's to blame; just trying to prevent it happening again"), my attitude belied my words. Why were they so defensive?

173

CHAPTER 5

Because I was so offensive. Now that the tables have turned,
I know how they felt. I am condemned by myself. The
children are giddy with the relief of the acquitted!

The apostle Paul advised Christians to "Let your
conversation be always full of grace" (Col. 4:6). The Greek
understanding of *conversation* extended beyond mere words
to one's entire manner of living.

I consider my daily "conversation" in light of this
incident. How does my manner of living conflict with my
intention of even my words? How often is my tone of voice
sharp or accusing? How often does my manner or posture
put my children on the defensive?

"Our children are our most important guests, who
enter into our home, ask for careful attention, stay for a
while and then leave to follow their own way," wrote Henri
Nouwen.[8] How would I treat my children if they were
"guests" in my home? Would I have handled the Scuff Case
differently if dinner guests were suspect? Do I offer to my
children the common courtesy I would extend to a stranger
or mere acquaintance? Is my manner of living seasoned with
grace?

My children are my most important guests. I must treat
them with dignity and respect. I must guard myself from
becoming so embroiled in the trivialities of daily maintenance that I fail to enjoy the pleasure of their company.


YOUR STORY
1. In what respect are our children "guests" in our homes?
2. Do you offer your children the same courtesy you
   would to any other guest in your home?

3. What prevents you from enjoying the pleasure of your children's companionship?
4. What can you do to improve your "conversation"—or manner of living—with your children?

# GUISE OF A STRANGER
# HOSPITALITY IS A MANDATE

*Rune of Hospitality*

I saw a stranger yestreen;
I put food in the eating place,
    Drink in the drinking place,
Music in the listening place;
    And in the blessed name of the Triune—
He blessed myself and my house,
    My cattle and my dear ones.
    And the lark said in her song
        Often, often, often,
Goes the Christ in the stranger's guise;
        Often, often, often,
Goes the Christ in the stranger's guise.[9]

Legends from many lands center around the theme of this old Gaelic poem: Christ appearing in the guise of a stranger. Perhaps nowhere is it related more poignantly than by Tolstoy in *Papa Panov's Special Day:*

Papa Panov was a shoemaker in a small Russian village. Content with his room, a stove, a firm bed, a little oil lamp, and enough customers to keep him busy, he was a happy man.

176

One Christmas Eve, however, alone in his room, he was overcome with memories of his wife who had died and his children who had gone away. Trying to take his mind off his lonely thoughts, he took a book off a shelf and began to read the story of Christmas. As he read how Jesus was born in a cowshed because there was no room at the inn, he wished they had come to him so he could have cared for the Christ child, maybe even giving Him a pair of tiny shoes.

He fell asleep reading only to be awakened by a voice: "Papa Panov. You wished that you had seen Me. I will come to you tomorrow. Be sure you recognize Me, for I shall not say who I am."

All Christmas long he eagerly awaited his guest. Others came by as was their custom—a roadsweeper, to whom he gave some coffee; a poor woman and her barefoot child whom he fitted with a pair of tiny shoes. Throughout the day people came by—to whom Papa Panov gave a coin, a hunk of bread, or a smile. But Jesus did not come.

As dusk fell he fought back tears, concluding the voice was just a dream. Then the same voice that he had heard on Christmas Eve spoke: "I was hungry and you gave Me food. I was thirsty and you gave Me water. I was cold and you took Me in. I did come, Papa Panov. These people you have helped today; all the time you were helping them you were helping Me."

Tolstoy's tale, like many other variations on this theme, finds its precedent in Scripture. Abraham and Sarah entertained three strangers only to discover that one of their guests was God in human form bringing the promise of a child to the incredulous elderly couple. Later in the Old Testament the Israelites strengthened and dignified the custom of gracious hospitality feeling that they, like Abraham, might be entertaining God in the guise of a stranger.

# CHAPTER 5

Christ extended this hope for everyone when He declared, "I tell you the truth, whatever you did for one of the least of these brothers of mine, you did for me" (Matt. 25:40).

A clear teaching of Christ carries tremendous implications for the ministry of hospitality. It influences whom we receive into our homes and why. Hospitality is lifted above mere personal gratification (arbitrary and optional) to a mandate of serious consideration. It forces us to stretch beyond our familiar comfort zones to the realm of sacrificial giving. Each act of caring viewed "as unto Christ" gains eternal significance.

What blocks us from opening the doors of our hearts and homes? Insecurity often inhibits us. We are uncertain as to whom we should invite, what we should serve, how we should proceed. Uneasy with our homes, perhaps, or our social skills, we postpone any invitation indefinitely. Overcrowded schedules likewise limit us. We have difficulty keeping up with our daily obligations, without the additional demands of hospitality. Limited in time and energy, we determine to do something later, at a better time . . . Sometimes we simply lack the desire to entertain. Secure in our routines and relationships, we are unwilling to be inconvenienced.

Through the years the role of hospitality in our home has been in a constant state of flux. My desire to have an open-house policy during Dave's early years of youth ministry resulted in an "energy crisis" that forced me to seek a more effective approach. Direction came in the pages of *L'Abri,* Edith Schaeffer's account of her family's radical ministry of hospitality. In this fascinating account she set forth sound principles that have guided me through the years. At the start she prayed that God would send the people of His choice to them—and keep the others away.

*L'Abri* forced me to examine my motives. Why was I permitting an unchecked siege of our home? Why couldn't I regulate the activity? I was challenged to seek God's direction in my choices and then trust Him for the necessary resources—spiritual and physical.

Second, Mrs. Schaeffer modeled a style of hospitality that was practical for me. Instead of allowing guests to halt her household tasks, she encouraged her visitors to join her in the kitchen while she cooked or ironed.

Wisely, she observed that a door has locks as well as hinges. Unless the door can be locked at certain times to nourish the family, the family will have little to offer one another or guests. (Recently this principle was tested when a woman, as dependent on caring people as on alcohol, arrived at our door moments after I had promised to read a story to Jonathan. I explained the situation to the insistent woman and then reported back to Jonathan. "Honey, I told her I could talk only ten minutes since you and I already have plans. I promise I'll be with you by the time you've finished your bath." His wet face beamed with pleasure as he said emphatically, "I know, 'cause *I'm* important, too.")

Hospitality is a privilege and a pleasure, the opportunity to share of one's bounty in the intimacy of friendship. Hospitality can be a ministry, a vehicle to embrace the needy or hurting in the nurturing womb of home. Regardless of motive, hospitality is a mandate for all who follow Christ. It is more an attitude than any given action: an opening of our hearts and homes to other people. It is a most expressive way of loving Christ and sharing Christ's love with others.

The role of hospitality is unique to each family and varies with life's changing circumstances. (I continue to struggle with the balance between locks and hinges.) Still, the principles are constant: We must prayerfully consider the concentric circles of caring beginning with our own family and broadening to include friends, neighbors, the hurting and needy, and yes—even the stranger. Then we must be responsive to God's leading, realizing that with each knock on our doors—literally and figuratively—comes the possibility that Christ awaits in the guise of a stranger.

## YOUR STORY

1. What blocks you from opening the doors of your home in hospitality? Time? Money? Lack of confidence or desire?
2. Do you know someone who needs to be embraced in the open arms of hospitality?
3. What is your growing edge in regard to hospitality: locks or hinges? What immediate measures could you take to correct this imbalance?

# CHAPTER 6
# WINDOW-SONGS:
# A PERSONAL VIEW

*An architect provides windows to frame the out-of-doors. Likewise a homemaker must develop vistas beyond her home to formulate a comprehensive worldview.*

# VIEW FROM MY WINDOW

*These vistas are developed by
exposure to a broad spectrum of
people, cultures, and ideas.*

For as long as I can remember, I have loved the view from
an upstairs window. My first bedroom possessed a second-
story dormer window. I loved to climb atop the little
dressing table snugly fitted into the tiny dormer space and
view the world from my lofty perch. Leaves, inaccessible at
ground level, were here within my reach, almost. Below me
I saw streets, sidewalks, and structures spread in panorama
diminished by distance. By carefully aligning my focus to
the slant of one rooftop, I could catch a glimpse of Park
Avenue, the magical link of the Concord Turnpike—main
street to Cambridge, to Boston, to everywhere.

The window in our present bedroom, likewise, has a
wonderful view. Leaves from great oaks brush against the
glass. My rooftop perspective of the neighborhood reveals a
delightful vista of dormers, gables, and chimneys. (At any
moment the soot-covered sweep from *Mary Poppins* could
come prancing around a chimney pot!) Seated at my desk, I
can see ducks waddling along the banks of idyllic Crystal
Lake, imperfections blurred from view. Our church steeple
pierces the sky, a daily reminder of the spiritual body that
has embraced our family for fifteen years. Beyond the little
lake rises the pale green water tower servicing this small

183

town that has become home to us. The street below drives a straight line across the railroad tracks into the heart of our downtown development—the boast and pride of the community. Beyond my view we are surrounded by citrus groves, the verdant setting for our town, "Crown Jewel of the Ridge."

In some ways windows are like the eyes of the house. We look out through them watching the rest of the world. From my upstairs window I have the advantage of increased perspective. Removed by height and distance, I gain a broader worldview, in the literal sense. My lofty isolation provides me a momentary, detached objectivity. It encourages a reflective solitude in which I can better sift through the clutter of my many selves; sort my thoughts, define my plans.

What do I see from my upstairs window? What do I gain from my lofty vista? I am reminded by steeple, tower, and highway that this home is the hub but not the limit of our lives. As snug as this dear hub may be, it serves as the connection for spokes that extend to the outer rim of our known world. Our goal must not be cozy insulation but participation and engagement with our church, community, and ultimately the greater world.

Also from my window I'm made cognizant of need, hurt, and prejudice. Pride in our refurbished downtown reminds me there remains a black town within a town still faltering in its efforts to integrate. The groves that fuel our prosperous citrus industry seasonally attract a migrant population hindered by illiteracy, rootlessness, and poverty. Our immediate neighborhood has been affected by the passage of time: Once-active citizens are now shut-ins; new families occupy the homes of the original town fathers, now passed on.

# VIEW FROM MY WINDOW

As I look upward out my window, through a canopy of trees I see patches of blue. I see glimpses of endless sky, domain of tiny birds in flight, of massive jets, of spaceships that hurdle beyond our atmosphere. Little me on a big Earth. Little Earth in a vast universe. My window reveals the enormity of things.

My window frames a view beyond the walls of home. It serves as a symbol, encouraging me to look beyond my home to gain a better perspective of myself, the world, and my place in the scheme of things. It forces me out of my ruts of complacency; it compels me to ask questions about my roles, my work, my relationship to the world.

Who am I? What is my identity when not defined by my roles of wife, mother, and homemaker? "Where are my lines then? my approaches? views? / Where are my window-songs?" asked poet George Herbert.

Through my window I converse with the world. I gain a truer sense of proportion. My window is a constant reminder of my continual need to withdraw from the business below, to quiet my heart, to open my mind to consider the vast vistas of living beyond this house. It underscores the necessity of rigorous thinking that leads to a comprehensive worldview. It challenges me to embrace life in all its fullness—temporal and eternal.

## YOUR STORY

1. What are your involvements beyond the walls of home?
2. What measures can you take to develop a broader perspective than your immediate environment? What enrichments can you pursue within the boundaries of your home?
3. What personal "ruts" potentially limit your development of a healthy, well-rounded worldview?

# BURDEN OF LIBERTY
# VISTAS OF OPTIONS

This is the first day of a new month. Taking the planning calendar from the kitchen door, I begin to place key events on the fresh, unmarked surface of March. I enter regular weekly and monthly commitments. Consulting the church and school calendars, I enter additional activities. I consult the children's sports schedules marking in David's home baseball games along with Jonathan's Little League games and Kimberly's tennis matches. I block off time for writing. As the month fills with activities, the remaining blank spaces become all the more precious.

Even as I consider the empty spaces rich with possibility, I can feel the month closing in on me. Soon our scheduled routines will be challenged by additional social and cultural offerings. The children's various activities invariably expand and conflict. Each remaining opening on the calendar represents choice. Each choice carries potential conflict.

How do we choose among the compelling options? Which activities should be given highest priority? What do we do when our individual events conflict? How involved should we be in the children's activities? When do we simply draw a line and say, "Enough"?

186

And what about my personal pursuits? The children's school day frees certain hours of the week to structure according to my desires. Yet faced with the many options, I find it difficult to choose. How much of that time should I devote to writing? What claim should church and community have on my free hours? How do I divide my time between home responsibilities and public service, between solitary and social activities?

Faced with the bewildering array of options, I am reminded of our cat's recent dilemma. Biscuit has the peculiar inclination to want to be where he isn't. When the door opens, he bounds from his location in the house and makes a dash for the door. If outside, he leaps up the porch stairs and races so rapidly over the threshold that he often skids across the wooden floor!

Several months ago the front door was removed from its hinges for repairs. As if on cue, Biscuit tore down the stairs and across the threshold to the great out-of-doors. Basking momentarily in his freedom, he observed the open door and raced back into the house. Before long, he felt once again compelled to make his break for freedom and dashed out onto the porch. He repeated this routine several more times. Finally he lay across the threshold—hind part in, front part out—in a total state of exhaustion.

Oh, the burden of liberty! Biscuit, like me, was exhausted by his freedom! How do I sift through the clutter of my many options? How do I determine my changing role with my constantly changing children? How do I resolve the tension between adult and family activities? On what basis do I make my choices? Are there guiding principles to determine my priorities? If I am not vigilant, I can spill away my precious time on meaningless activities that leave me depleted and the family unguarded.

# CHAPTER 6

"Almost every woman I know is too busy," maintains psychologist Robert A. Johnson. "She is into this, studying that, driving in a carpool to this and that, working hard on some big project, racing around until she is ragged."[1] Somewhere we women have gained the idea that we can do it all. Drawn to the rich possibilities of life, we wish to do them all at once. Even as we are doing one thing, we are considering another. The problem is that it doesn't work. We can't do it all and do it well. Something suffers, sometimes our families, often ourselves.

Johnson looks to the ancient myth of Amor and Psyche for answers for modern women. One of the tasks given Psyche by Aphrodite as a condition for her deliverance, or wholeness, is the impossible assignment of filling a crystal goblet with water from the river Styx. Almost inaccessible, the Styx tumbles from a high mountain into the earth and goes back to the mountain again. Any exposed stretches are guarded by dangerous monsters. An eagle sent by Zeus comes to Psyche's distress, takes the crystal goblet, flies to the center of the stream, lowers the goblet into the turbulent waters, fills it, and brings it safely back to Psyche.

The lesson of the crystal goblet is that women need to be quiet, to approach the vastness of life in a more orderly manner, to do one thing—take one crystal goblet at a time—concentrate on it, and do it well. Then she may move on to other things.

The application of this lesson for me is twofold: It tells me to quiet my soul and do what I have to do right now with singleness of mind. It also encourages me to focus on the activities unique to this particular stage in my life, to save for another time what can wait so I can devote myself to what cannot.

The crystal goblet represents choice. Like the eagle who

188

has panoramic vision, I must survey the vast river of options, focus on the most essential object, and dip out a single goblet of water. Choice invariably requires sacrificing one good thing for a better thing. It sometimes means sacrificing oneself for another.

The critical consideration for my choices at this point in life is the family. The children's time at home is limited. I don't want to fumble the ball in the last inning. Ironically at the very moment I am liberated by additional time to explore independent interests, my children are most consciously forming their own identities. Most of the time they are independently occupied. Often they seem indifferent, even resistant, to my involvement in their lives. Yet just when it seems my time might be more productive elsewhere, something happens that requires my presence. I want to be there when my children need me. In the words of Emily Dickinson,

> They may not need me—
> Yet they might—
> I'll keep my heart just in sight—
> A smile like mine might be
> Precisely their necessity—

I'm not ready to conclude that I must ignore my own development or interests. Yet I'm not willing to pursue my interests at the expense of the family. There are, of course, many wonderful compensations at this stage of life. And contrary to the contemporary message of society, I believe that as I give to others, I am becoming more fully myself. It is a spiritual paradox: In giving we receive; in losing we gain; in dying we are born.

It is a noble calling to mediate between home and the

world for my husband and for my children. At those rare moments when I am truly denying myself of something dear for this higher good, I'm bolstered by the belief that even as I build the home for others, *I* am being built from within. The master Architect strengthens and refines each one of us through sacrifice; He stretches and broadens us through giving.

> Blest be the Architect whose art
> Could build so strong in a weak heart.
> —George Herbert

## YOUR STORY

1. What are your most important responsibilities at this point in your life? Is their importance revealed through your choices of how you spend your time, energy, and money?
2. What are your involvements beyond your responsibilities?
3. Which activities create the greatest stress in your life? Could any of these be postponed to a later time?
4. Which activities provide the greatest nourishment to your life?

# BELLE LETTRES
## VISTAS OF FRIENDSHIP

The *World Book Dictionary* defines *belle lettres* as "beautiful writing; the finer forms of literature." I find that personal correspondence is one of the most fascinating categories of the fine art of writing. The list lengthens of those with whom I assume intimacy—because I have read their mail! Through volumes containing correspondence of decades, the reticent Anne Morrow Lindbergh revealed insight into the people and events of her rich life. Scholar C. S. Lewis revealed the warm personal aspect of his domestic life through personal letters. Dietrich Bonhoeffer offered a rare perspective of private and world affairs in his correspondence from a Nazi prison. And for the true romantic, what can surpass the love letters of Robert Browning and Elizabeth Barrett?

Flannery O'Connor, Chekhov, Sylvia Plath—I have traveled to faraway places with them, endured the petty frustrations of their domestic lives, shared their joys, sorrows, worries, and frets. I have mused with them about life, agonized and triumphed with their writing careers.

My love of reading others' mail is secondary, however, to receiving mail of my own! Knowing full well that each delivery brings its share of bills, advertisements, even bad news, I always feel expectant and excited at the sight of our mailman rounding the corner with his leather bag chock full of who knows what! Eagerly I sort through the offerings in search of a particular postmark or familiar script. What news, revelations, messages, treasures, or intimacies might lie within the sealed envelopes?

"Letters are small gifts that call attention precisely to their writer as well as to the subjects the writer pens round," wrote Lee Hall.[2] However packaged, be it a detailed chronicle of daily activities or a brief note on a Christmas card, I always welcome communication from a friend.

Some people have developed this form of communication to a fine art. One octogenarian begins his letter with "Good Morning!" and proceeds to jot down what is on his mind at that moment as if continuing a conversation from the previous day. His last letter listed his favorite quotations collected throughout decades of reading.

Another elderly friend takes up her pen on sleepless nights. A recent communication jotted on the back of used paper—her contribution to recycling efforts—included the time (3:00 A.M.), a description of her setting ("Wrapped in a knitted shawl in a chair pulled up to a little woodburning stove, sipping hot chocolate"), a poem she composed ("Miriam, is this worth entering in a contest as poetry?"), some memories about "dear Nels," and several current newspaper clippings. A puffy envelope from Anne could include anything from a pocketful of autumn leaves to recipes and quotations culled from her files.

One friend's occasional letters are well worth the wait. She sends fascinating packets of assorted treasures—like photographs, a small article of clothing for a child, reading lists, highlights from the intervening years—all within a beautiful art card.

Another friend, who is a perennial world traveler, has mastered the geometrics of the postcard. On the backs of picturesque cards addressed to "The Rock-Nest," he manages to convey intimate glimpses of place as well as his own personal spirit.

Mother, chief of "cliptomaniacs," gathers material culled from newspapers, magazines, books, and programs, periodically shipping them fourth class in manila envelopes. Within these current "scrapbooks" of my parents' lives Mother includes her personal commentary: a chatty letter in fine script explaining and elaborating the contents.

What will the mailman bring today? Who knows? But in days past, along with bills, ads, and catalogs, have been wonderful surprises: an apt cartoon from a local resident, a cassette tape of music or monologue, a hand-crocheted collar tucked inside a birthday card, a greeting from a college friend, an epistle catching me up on missing months.

As for myself I must confess that I have more good intentions than written letters. I collect stationery along with scribblings and clippings that I intend to include—when I write. I envision a future time when I will reserve a portion of each day exclusively for correspondence. I will contact friends of the past, thank the people who have guided or encouraged me, write the authors who have nourished me, send the photo, pictures, or clipping to a friend, pen the word of encouragement to a weary spirit. Meanwhile the stack builds up, attended at moments of random inspiration or absolute necessity.

Failure notwithstanding, I recognize the value of the heartfelt note—the true belle lettres of the writing world. The U.S. Postal Service announces from time to time an increase in the cost of stamps. I never complain. Five cents, twelve cents, fifteen cents, twenty-two cents, twenty-five cents . . . small price to pay for services rendered: the winging of letter over land and sea. For the small price of postage, old friendships are nourished and maintained, new friendships are established and cultivated.

The next time I'm tempted to "reach out and touch someone," I must pause before picking up the phone. I must consider: Is now the time to pick up, instead, a pen and some paper and offer that person a *permanent* proof of caring—a belle lettre of the heart?

## YOUR STORY

1. In what ways do friends broaden one's worldview?
2. What friendships have been the most challenging to your way of thinking?
3. How do you react when a friend differs from your point of view?
4. What are you currently doing to nourish your friendships?

# WINDOWS OF THE MIND
## VISTAS OF THOUGHT

*A house without books is like a*
*room without windows.*
                    *—Thomas Mann*

Books grace each room of our house like the friendly faces of people who grace my life. As with friends, each book has a special place in my heart and mind. Certain books, like certain friends, happen to be in view at the right time with the right word for a particular need, informing my thinking, which in turn informs the very direction of my life. Other books vary in degree of closeness and influence, ranging from nodding acquaintance to intimate companions.

A walk through our house offers a cursory introduction to these friends. We put our best foot forward in the living room, hosting the lives and works of those who have endured the test of time in art, literature, and music: oversized art books (old masters and lyrical impressionists); exquisitely illuminated facsimiles of the *Book of Hours*; collected works of Robert Louis Stevenson, Shakespeare, O. Henry, Emily Dickinson, and Robert Frost. Hardbound volumes of piano literature and stiff-backed chorale scores share shelves with stacks of sheet music representative of centuries of vocal and instrumental compositions. Memoirs of Edward Bok share space with memorabilia from Bok Tower Gardens, his wonderful gift to America.

Mingled amongst this eclectic gathering are beautifully

195

bound out-of-print editions unearthed in secondhand book shops: slim volumes of poetry bound in delicately colored covers with titles stamped in gold—Tennyson, Wordsworth, Lowell, and Keats—plus handsome leather-bound, gold-embossed essays of Emerson, Ruskin, Scott, and Arnold.

On a table in the stairway landing rests a red soft-leather volume with gleaming gold letters, *The Light of Faith* by Edgar A. Guest. An inscription from houseguests refers to a particular page with a house blessing titled, "Lines for a Friend's House."

At the top of the stairs an ample bookcase houses helpful resource books for personal and family living. Here reside trusted old friends who have guided me through crossroads and crises—Paul Tournier, Catherine Marshall, Elisabeth Elliot, James Dobson, Edith Schaeffer, John Stott, and C. S. Lewis—among others. Flannery O'Connor, Eudora Welty, Ranier Rilke, and other writers await with ready advice on the creative process. A row of Elizabeth Goudge novels line a top shelf, reminding me of comfortable English domesticity and noble Anglican sensibility. Dozens of other acquaintances crowd the remaining space, preserving their unique contributions for a moment's notice.

Stuffed animals and wooden toys hold sentinel guard in built-in bookcases on the adjacent wall. Jemima Puddleduck and Benjamin Bunny keep a sharp eye on Beatrix Potter's menagerie of dressed animals in their shiny white-glazed book jackets. Raggedy Ann and Andy are wedged between my beloved childhood companions—Anne of Green Gables and Louisa May Alcott's classics—and my children's discoveries, Lewis's world of Narnia and *The Little House on the Prairie* books. Throughout these hallowed shelves, *The Illustrated Mother Goose* and all manner of picture books mix comfortably with the young-adult fiction of Madeleine L'Engle and Katherine Paterson.

In a large wooden cupboard on the sitting room wall are books with a "house" motif. Architectural and decorating sourcebooks—*The Cranbrook Vision, English Style, French Country*—stand alongside instructional resources about homemaking—*Hidden Art; What Is a Family?; Open Heart, Open Home.*

Scattered throughout our bedroom is current reading material. Stacked on our respective sides of the bed are unread volumes Dave and I intend to read; piled on desk and file tops are resources for study and writing projects. We keep alive the dream of a trip to England by a growing collection of travel guides and books about the English countryside and by British authors. Our marital ideals are nourished by the sight of two volumes on a bedside shelf— the Bible covered in mother-of-pearl that I carried down the aisle on our wedding day and a dainty white leather book with pages edged in gold, *Affectionate Advice to a Married Couple,* dated 1886. From enticing offerings, from Van Loon's historical *Lives* to John McPhee's contemporary study *Oranges* to M. F. K. Fisher's *Among Friends* to Isak Dinesen's *Winter Tales,* I'm certain never to be bored—if I can stay awake!

Downstairs, wedged between rolls of wrapping paper and ribbons in the hallway cupboard, I store reference books on marbling, collages, and other paper works to lure me from practical to leisurely pursuits.

Even the bathroom houses a growing library of "privy literature," including *The Classic Outhouse Book.* Never a wasted moment!

*The Joy of Cooking* and the *Better Homes and Gardens*

# CHAPTER 6

*Cook Book* head the books of recipes that crowd kitchen shelves and spill over into the dining room.

Treasured devotional classics rest on my prayer bench shelf: daily readings from Amy Carmichael's letters and poetry, Oswald Chambers' *My Utmost for His Highest,* Mrs. Cowman's *Streams in the Desert,* plus prayer books and hymnals. On the kneeling bench I've laid the gradually acquired works of my beloved Lilias Trotter. Manor-born Lilias disappointed her mentor John Ruskin by abandoning England and a career in art to minister to Muslims in North Africa. Out of a life of devotion to God and service to the Arab people, she composed her exquisitely illustrated *Parables of the Cross* and *Parables of the Christ-Life.* The very sight of her books, jacketed in plain khaki paper with beautiful black lettering, inspires me anew with the example of Miss Trotter's faith, life, and art.

A wide variety of friends have congregated on the shelf-lined wall of the morning room. East meets the West on a shelf of short stories and novels by authors such as Chekhov and Dostoyevski, Jane Austen and Henry James.

And then there are the shelves of books whose sole link is quite simply that I love them. Dear friends to me, I wonder how they might mix with each other? I can't help but feel that these friends, however diverse in background or viewpoint, would respond as I to the special insight or beauty that makes me value this eclectic gathering. Surely, though differing in worldviews, the urbane Lord Kenneth Clark or erudite Isaiah Berlin would willingly profit from the otherworldly wisdom of the desert fathers or Saint Francis. Differing as they did in lifestyles, Christina Rossetti would not object to her soft leather-bound collection of devotional verse being placed next to the small hardcover edition of critical essays about the pre-Raphaelite art of her brother Dante Rossetti.

Books, indeed, are friends. They are frigates that carry us to far reaches of earth and space—past, present, and future. They are letters of introduction to people of distinction or acclaim. Books are hallowed halls of learning in which we confer with sages and philosophers, scientists and poets. Books are magic gateways to wonder, beauty, and delight. They broaden our worldviews through places, people, and experiences otherwise inaccessible to us. They sharpen our minds and fire our imaginations on the thought, wit, and humor of the savant. Our hearts are quickened and emotions stirred with experiences within their pages that probe the depths of human experience. They increase our understanding of ourselves and empathy with others by exposing us to situations we have not yet encountered. Books convey values, ideals, and truth in the context of real life. They give "wings to the spirit," liberating us from the physical boundaries that limit us. In short, books make up the difference in our experience.

Yes, books are friends that people our home. As I walk through the rooms of this house, titles and authors greet me from their narrow spines and colorful jackets, recalling past experience, offering new adventure. From this printed society I can choose at will the perfect companion for the moment, to divert or delight, to challenge or to soothe, to provide a touchstone with life's pressing realities, or to offer instead an escape. Surrounded with such accommodating companions, I need never be lonely or bored; I need never be confined or limited. Books, indeed, are friends. They are windows that open endless vistas, beyond my furthest reach or imagining!

# CHAPTER 6

All that mankind has done, thought, gained or been: It is lying as in magic preservation in the pages of books. They are the choicest possessions of men.

—Thomas Carlyle

## YOUR STORY

1. In what ways are books like windows?
2. What are you doing to stretch the boundaries of your mind?
3. What goals do you have for your personal development? What plans do you have for achieving your goals?

# ICON CORNER
## VISTAS OF THE SOUL

In her book *The Kitchen Madonna*, Rumer Godden relates the story of Gregory, an aloof and silent boy. Gregory and his younger sister were left largely in the care of a succession of maids to whom they were indifferent—until Marta. Responding to the warmth and stability that Marta brought to their fine London house, Gregory was deeply distressed that she was unhappy. Fearing she would leave, Gregory uncharacteristically extended himself to find out the source of her unhappiness. Reluctantly she admitted that their home, though modern and efficient, had no "good place" such as she had once had in her Ukranian kitchen. Pressed as to the nature of this "good place," Marta haltingly explained, "In my home we make a good place. In the corner, there a place on top of cupboard, perhaps, or perhaps on shelf. Little place but it holy because we keep there Our Lady and Holy Child."[3]

As Marta continued to describe the good place, Gregory conceived an idea. How Gregory came to understand her need and tried to fill it, how he went through one difficulty and disappointment after another to purchase an icon of the Madonna, and how he finally succeeded by a creative act of his own is the whole of this simple story. Yet

201

in this singular tale the author underscores the human need to have tangible touchstones for intangible realities.

I, too, have a good place from which I derive encouragement and support. In one corner of the dining room I've placed a chair and the prayer bench given to Dave upon graduation from seminary. Over the prayer bench is a collage of pictures, texts, and objects of spiritual significance. I ascribe no actual value to my "icon corner," but, like Marta's "good place," it provides visual reassurance of the foundational truths it represents; artists' conceptions of Christ's birth, death, and resurrection; texts and symbols of scriptural teaching about the life of faith—prayer, service, and love.

The inspiration for my icon corner is John Wesley's prayer room, as depicted on a postcard hung in the lower left of the collage. The room, bare but for a table, chair, and kneeling bench, was called the "power house of Methodism." Wesley said of this room: "Here then am I, far from the busy ways of men. I sit down alone, only God is here."

On a college trip to England, keenly frustrated with my own lack of spiritual vitality, I visited John Wesley's home. Claiming no special victory or attributes as witness to my faith, I stood before this barren room in which John Wesley had spent the first hours of each day; a truth suddenly broke over me like a beam of light: My desire for the benefits of the Christian life had preempted the primary goal: knowing God. I had desired the gifts more than the Giver. God was saying, "Want *Me*. Get to *know* Me. All the rest will follow." In the stillness of that moment I resolved to put first things first: to spend time alone with God, learning to know Him, learning to love Him. I purchased a postcard of this room as a reminder of my commitment.

Through the years there have been other moments of

illumination, little epiphanies, as the mystics call them, episodes in which God revealed His truth to me in a special way. Likewise, I have selected objects to represent these truths—icons of a sort—symbols of a spiritual reality: a watercolor of a woman reposing on a garden bench (a reminder to carve from each day a slice of solitude and hem it in with quietness); a small pottery cup, reminding me that any act of caring is regarded by Christ as a "cup of cold water" given to Him; a crystal sparkling with refracted light, symbolizing the new quality brought to the human soul by the light of God's sanctifying love. These simple objects and many others provide daily reminders of God's unchanging truth, stones of remembrance for my forgetful heart.

Important as each new discovery may be in my walk of faith, none has transcended that lesson gained before that English room so many years ago: There is nothing on earth as important as knowing God. Now when I rush about my daily rounds, caught up in the all-consuming business of the moment, my little space—my icon corner—is a vivid reminder: "Be still, and know that I am God" (Ps. 46:10).

My icons, though not intrinsically sacred, do provide invaluable reminders to this wayward heart of mine. They shed light on the pilgrim pathway of my journey to my heavenly home.

## YOUR STORY

1. What is your relationship with God?
2. In what ways can you see evidences of His involvement in your life?
3. What are you doing to cultivate a personal relationship with God?
4. If you are not a believer in Christ, what efforts are you making to discover Truth?

# THROUGH EYES OF FAITH
## VISTAS UNTO ETERNITY

Placing the phone on the receiver, my mind reels with the impact of the message of this long-distance call. In a flat tone of voice my friend informed me that her cancer has spread from the lymph system into the bones. One cell gone wild— dividing and multiplying at such speed and tenacity that even a six-month assault of the strongest chemicals could not halt its relentless progress. What lies ahead for Kia? For years we have discussed our mutual concerns about child rearing; we have shared our hopes and dreams for our children. Now she asks, "Will I see my children grow up? Will my baby even remember me?"

By what caprice of chance or design has my friend been singled out for this devastation? What kind of a world do we live in, anyway? Today's headlines flash into my head: Bombing in the Middle East; "wars and rumors of wars. . . ." Smaller print on the front page estimates the number of people killed by a tornado that stormed the northeastern coastline; "famine and earthquakes. . . ." Smaller captions promise details of a drug bust on the west coast of the state; murder in South Florida; "many . . . will betray and hate each other . . ." (see Matt. 24:6–10).

Suddenly all the headlines and fine print become

individuals who, like Kia, have friends and family who love them, who likewise are ravished by the pain and loss of this not very nice world. Those soldiers in military garb could be my sons; that hapless victim, my daughter; those families eliminated by the chance current could be ours.

How does one put it all together? How does one find explanations for what appears to be totally arbitrary devastation and disaster? Throughout all time humans have attempted to make sense of things. We have looked to countless sources for answers to life's troublesome enigmas.

The Christian—or any honest and open seeker—must search Scripture for explanations. The Bible alone, I'm convinced, adequately addresses the full range of human experience. As one studies the entire sweep of Scripture, one gains a sense of the whole: creation as God intended it; human freedom to voluntarily submit to God's plan; the inevitable consequence of our rebellion, our brokenness, pain, death, alienation from God and one another; God's redemptive plan unfolded through the nation of Israel and fulfilled through Christ's death; the eventual establishment of a new order with the passing of the old—a new creation where God will dwell in unbroken fellowship with His children, where there will be no more death or mourning or crying or pain. As we examine the details of God's dealings with individuals through Old and New Testament history, we gain a true understanding of ourselves and of our relationship to God and humankind: God's desire to relate personally to us to direct us daily by the set boundaries of His laws, by His guiding rule of love, and by the gentle nudging of His Holy Spirit. As we steep and ground ourselves in God's Word, we develop a biblical viewpoint— a truly comprehensive understanding of this world and eternity.

# CHAPTER 6

When as a young adult I first became convinced that the Bible was God's divine revelation, I wanted to read it. Where, then, should I begin? At the beginning, of course. I began in Genesis, fully intending to read straight through to Revelation. How many times did I begin Genesis only to get bogged down in Chapter 10 with the "begats" of Noah's sons? I tried the time-proven through-the-Bible-in-one-year plan of reading two chapters in the Old Testament and one in the New Testament only to be overwhelmed with so much material that I fell helplessly behind and concluded that I would begin again—next year! I tried reading single books of the Bible or topical studies, a Proverb a day or random verses.

Not until I embarked upon a dated systematic Bible reading program did I begin to feel that I was slowly and surely developing a comprehensive understanding of God's Word.[4] By following the designated passages, I was able to read the entire Bible in a sequential pattern over five years. The manageable segments permitted time to meditate on the meaning of the passage, to ask questions and search answers, to consider the personal application. Bolstered with a cup of coffee, a notebook, and planning calendar to jot down practical insights or specific plans for the day, I can integrate Scripture with my daily doings as I meditate on the Word and God's point of view.

Learning to view the world in the light of Scripture is a slow process. It involves rethinking concepts accepted by society; it requires a painful examination of motives and actions. Some things we simply won't understand. Others we'll struggle to accept. We will never tap the inexhaustible resources in the Word.

There is much in this world I don't understand. I have no satisfactory explanation for my friend or myself. I place

206

my trust, nonetheless, in my all-seeing Master who answered the questioning Job,

> Brace yourself like a man;
>     I will question you,
> and you shall answer me.
>     Where were you when I laid the earth's
>         foundation? (Job 38:3–4)

and then proceeded to enumerate His creations, from the whimsical ostrich to immense constellations. I, like Job, can only respond,

> Surely I spoke of things I did not understand,
>     things too wonderful for me to know. . . .
> My ears had heard of you
>     but now my eyes have seen you. (Job 42:3, 5)

Our "eyes of faith" must turn from the questions that cannot be answered to the God who can be known. The bottom line is an issue of faith: Have we a Master we can trust? An affirmative answer makes all the difference.

My room has a window with a view. From my window I see distortion and devastation alongside beauty and joy. I see through a glass darkly, but I see through the eyes of faith. Now I know in part. Someday I will see my Master face to face. Then I shall know fully: All will be clear; all will be satisfied. But for the time being I must content myself with the light of Scripture, the joy of Christ's indwelling presence, and occasional glimpses of eternity.

> And now these three remain: faith, hope and love.
> But the greatest of these is love. (1 Cor. 13:13)

# CHAPTER 6

## YOUR STORY

1. Does your worldview include an eternal dimension?
2. How does the perspective of eternity affect your view of life on earth? Why is this so important?
3. In what ways can you strengthen your "eyes of faith"?

# CHAPTER 7
# THE ROAD BY MY DOOR:
# GROWING UP TO GO AWAY

*An architect plans a roadway to the world beyond the house. A homemaker plans the transition to maturity knowing full well that the very path that leads children home each day will someday lead them away.*

# THE ROAD LEADS ON

*Preparation for maturity requires the*
*gradual transition from dependency*
*to autonomy.*

"See ya, Mom. Remember, my game starts at six!"

Jonathan, dressed in full uniform, turns briefly to wave, then heads down the driveway toward the ballpark. Alone again at home, I consider how many of the children's waking hours are lived beyond the four walls of our house. Even during the summer the children are constantly on the move—away at camp or Bible school, off to the baseball fields or tennis courts, to friends' homes or part-time jobs. All day long the hours are punctuated with the comings and goings of children.

Even as I anticipate the children's return each day, I feel a sharp tug at my heart: Each indication of increased independence is a reminder that they are growing up to go away. The same road that leads them away from home and back again each day will someday take them away forever.

Gazing at the quiet road by my door, I'm reminded of an incident related by a son of Carson Callaway, creator of the lovely Callaway Gardens. Throughout Howard's childhood the family drove muddy roads, car loaded with children and dogs, to their isolated property on the northern slopes of Pine Mountain, Georgia. "Once a stranger . . . pulled up in front of the house," wrote Howard. "He called to my father, 'Hey Mister, where does this road go?' 'Mexico city,' my father answered without cracking a smile. 'No it don't,' the visitor said. 'Yes, it does,' my father said. 'If I was going to leave here to go to Mexico City that's the road I'd take.'"[1]

*Where does this road go?* I wonder. *Where will it take my children?* It goes to ballparks, local schools, and summer jobs. It goes on and on to weekend retreats, summer camps, and out-of-state colleges. The same road leading through our sleepy town connects to Highway 27, a north-south artery through the USA. The road by my door, which leads them home each day, is taking them farther and farther away, to their final destination: independence.

That movement toward maturity brings inevitable challenges. Truly the transition from dependency to autonomy is uncharted territory. Greater freedom for child spells less control for parent. Although the shift from child to adult is gradual, each new decision is fraught with uncertainty. Be it dating or driving, use of time or money, issues academic or extracurricular—the greater the choices, the greater the consequences. In the decisions that lie ahead—education, vocation, location, and matrimony—the stakes are high!

Amid the daily challenges in this transitional stage, I must face the ultimate challenge of preparing the children to leave home. Questions haunt me: Will they be ready to face adult responsibilities? Will I be ready to let them go?

I recall an incident a friend related several years ago. One morning her neighbor phoned. "Come quickly," she insisted without explanation. Immediately my friend rushed next door to discover her neighbor in the backyard. "Look," she instructed, pointing to an overhead tree limb. Cradled in the fork was a nest. A mother bird was trying to push the last of her brood out. Push as she would, the bird would not

212

budge. Finally, as the women watched, the mother bird began to disassemble the nest! She poked and pulled at the twigs, leaves, and grass of the snug shelter in which the little bird huddled, until the nest gave way. The women held their breath as the fledgling dropped, dropped, dropped, then fluttered its wings—and flew!

Despite my emotional ambivalence, there are no options: Someday my fledglings must leave home, ready or not. To postpone departure serves neither the parents nor the child. Erik Erickson, observing modern Western society's tendency to prolong childhood, has noted: "It is human to have a long childhood; it is civilized to have an ever longer childhood. Long childhood makes a technical and mental virtuoso out of man, but it also leaves a lifelong residue of emotional immaturity in him."[2]

The inevitable transition from childhood to adulthood involves certain death—for both the child and the parent. The child must, in the words of 1 Corinthians 13:11, "put away childish things" (KJV); the child must die to dependencies and familiar securities. The parent must let go not only of the child but of a very special phase of life. Each experiences an acute sense of loss.

Renunciation—the willing and graceful sacrifice of that which has served its rightful purpose—is a fundamental aspect of living. It is a natural law: "Death is the gate of life."[3] The dark night of winter is requisite to the birth of spring. So it is with the seasons of human life. Each phase has its appointed time. We must live fully each age and stage—then die to it that we might progress to the next level. Any attempt to prolong any relationship—with person, place, stage, or thing—is counterproductive. "We mortals die many deaths in our lives," wrote Virginia Stem Owens.

Patterns that have served the purposes of their particular time and place have to be discarded and left behind. If we grow in wisdom and stature, it is only over the dead bodies of our former selves. One cannot begin to live a new life until the old one has adequately died. Otherwise life itself becomes nothing but an artificial resuscitation, year after year, of a desiccated, worn-out self, a mummy with only the painted appearance of life.[4]

In the words of Solomon, "There is a time for everything, and a season for every activity under heaven" (Eccl. 3:1).

Of course there have already been many little deaths in the season of motherhood, beginning with the initial separation of birth. One might say that each "first" is a warm-up exercise in relinquishment: weaning, baby-sitter, visit away from home, morning at nursery school, overnight at a friend's, week at camp, solo driving, single dating. But there is no doubt in my heart that none of these compares to the final relinquishment of my children when they leave home. Everything in my heart resists.

Yet even as I lament "letting go," I recognize indications of the birth of a new stage. Decreased need for supervision brings greater freedom for me. Fewer physical demands from the children releases more time for me and with Dave. Increasingly the children contribute to the common welfare of the home. As I delight in their emerging personalities revealed through their interests, conversations, and accomplishments, I anticipate enjoyment in my young adult companions—yes, friends.

So I look down the road past my door, the road that leads Jonathan to his ball game, the road that will someday

take each child across town to the main artery to anywhere. . . .

I will not stop them. Rather, in their remaining years at
home, I will direct my energies toward equipping them for
the road. Together Dave and I will teach them to love "the
road" with its varied songs and cadences, so that each in the
appointed time can claim the words of Walt Whitman:

Afoot and light-hearted I take to the open road,
   Healthy, free, the world before me,
The long brown path before me leading wherever I
   choose.

## YOUR STORY

1. In "letting go" of your children what immediate
   challenges do you face?
2. What "little deaths" or relinquishments with your
   children have you already faced?
3. How does the ultimate goal of total independence for
   your children affect decisions you are making today?

# SOLILOQUY ON A SLEEPING BOY
# PREPARATION FOR GROWING UP

*I sigh that kiss you,*
*For I must own.*
*That I shall miss you*
*When you have grown.*[5]

"You go on to bed. I'll be up in a minute to tuck you in," I call to Jonathan.

"Okay," answers a sleepy voice.

A phone call later I ascend the stairs to perform the nightly ritual.

"Ready?" I ask, walking into his bedroom. A sleeping form is sprawled across the bed. Light from the hallway illumines a face rendered cherubic by slumber. On one side of him lies the furry bulk of his teddy bear, companion from early childhood; on the other side, cradled in the crook of his arm, is a baseball mitt, symbol of increased independence. The golden-haired child clad in a long white nightshirt—his father's softball jersey—could be a slumbering angel.

Sleeping boy, what are you? One moment you're an independent little man, heading off to the ball field, challenging bedtimes and boundaries, doing everything in your power to claim the time-earned stature of your older siblings. The next moment you're a cuddly child snuggling up to teddy, pleading for a bedtime story, hanging on to your status as "baby" of the family.

What are you, little one? You are still a child, but not for long. I treasure each day, knowing that your passage into the no-man's-land of preadolescence is not only the end of childhood for you—but also for me. How I'd love to stop the clock and hold you forever at this enchanting stage—keep you forever the lovely child before me to hug and cuddle and to indulge the undying child in me.

But I can't. Not at the risk of creating a resident Peter Pan, ever child in Never-Never Land. No, the challenges of this stage are too great to acquiesce to sheer sentiment. How easy it is with you, the youngest, to follow the path of least resistance: to relax the rules or the discipline, to overlook important childhood experiences or allow the elder family members to carry the load while you coast. I must be vigilant to your requirements as a child while you push and strain for added liberty and privileges.

I can't stop the clock, but I will turn this soliloquy into new resolve for your remaining days of childhood. I resolve to preserve the quiddity of childhood for you, Jonathan, to cultivate daily the disciplines and delights of this special stage of your life. I will savor each moment, relishing your hugs and kisses, your uncensored confidences, your unjaded vision of this wonder-filled world. And when the days of childhood draw to a close, I will release you to the next phase with confidence knowing, "First the child, then the man."

So good night, little one. Cherish each day as I cherish you.

## YOUR STORY

1. Why is an unhurried childhood so important to a child's development?
2. What factors push your child to grow up too fast?
3. In what areas of child rearing do you need to be more vigilant?

# AN OPEN LETTER TO KIMBERLY
# PREPARATION FOR WOMANHOOD

Dear Kimberly,

Three years ago, on your tenth birthday, I gave you the amethyst ring given to me when I was ten. Remembering that your first ring had been a reminder of your parents' love, you asked, "What does *this* ring mean?" After some thought, I answered, "Purple is a royal color. Let this ring remind you that you are God's child—a daughter of a King!"

To mark your turning teen, your father and I give you an amethyst stone on a golden chain. When you wear this necklace, let it remind you that you are a King's daughter with all the rights and privileges of a princess: royal status, estate, and inheritance and access to the King.

You have long been fascinated with royalty. You awakened before dawn to watch the royal wedding of Prince Charles and Lady Diana, an event having all the majesty and magic of a fairy tale. You have a growing collection of books and articles about Princess Diana—the embodiment of a young girl's dream of feminine beauty.

This week Prince Charles and Princess Diana make their first royal visit to the States. Once again the market is flooded with royal lore. Lovely Diana graces the covers of magazines. Articles dissect and analyze every known detail of their marriage and family, not to mention public appearances and personal possessions. One article is devoted entirely to the jewels she received since her engagement to the prince. A sapphire engagement ring was Prince Charles's first gift to his future bride. His wedding gift was a pendant of the Prince of Wales' three-feather motif done in diamonds. Diana's first royal heirloom was a tiara with nineteen large pearls suspended below lover's knots of diamonds, given by Queen Elizabeth. She was also given an emerald and diamond choker that once belonged to Queen Mary.

The word *gem* is taken from the Latin word *gemma,* meaning "bud."

Today we celebrate the significant rite of passage into your teen years—those transitional years from the bud of childhood to the full bloom of womanhood. I can't help but recall with nostalgia other significant landmarks of growth—your first steps, starting school, the shearing of your ponytails into a fashionable wedge, entering junior high school. Surely, turning teen deserves full fanfare.

If I could, I would give to you precious gems to mark this special occasion and to adorn your lovely person. Instead I will remind you of these gems' priceless properties.

I would give you gold for truthfulness. Gold is a favored metal to shape into settings for valuable jewels. The glowing beauty of gold is achieved by subjecting the precious metal to the refiner's fire, in which all that is false is melted and purged. May you love the truth in all things. May it produce in you fidelity to God and to His commands that are "more precious than gold, than much pure gold" (Ps. 19:10), insight into yourself, integrity in your dealings with others.

I would give you diamonds for strength of character. Diamonds are the hardest and most enduring natural substance. May you develop the strength to meet each of life's challenges: endurance through stress and hardship; courage to hold firm to your convictions, to risk the unknown; steadiness like a rooted tree, not disturbed by storm or winds of passing thought and fashion. To acquire the greatest possible brilliance, the diamond is sundered in half by the craftsman's skilled blow, then carefully polished. Know that in the skillful hands of your Father, all life's stinging blows and disappointments will be redeemed, rendering shape, radiance, and brilliance to your life.

I would give you rubies for individuality. Rubies, rich, red, and beautiful, are highly valued for their rarity. May you be certain of your rarity as a unique creation of God. There is no other person like yourself. You were an idea in the mind of God before you were conceived. May this knowledge give you the right blend of confidence and humility: confidence that, as a creation of God, you are special; humility in that all your attributes are gifts from your Creator to be used according to His design and purpose. May you come to a perfect acceptance of who you are—finding strength from God in your weakness; finding expression of your strength in service to others.

I would give you emeralds for growth. Emeralds are valued for their rich green color. Green, in legend and liturgy, symbolizes growth. May you always live on the growing edge of your life, not resting in natural talent or past success, not blocked by dogmatism or prejudice. One never stands still. May you nourish your mind with poetry and good books and season it with lively conversation; may you nourish your spirit with great music, art, and drama;

may you nourish your soul with mysteries and sureties, with praises and with prayer.

I would give you pearls for purity. Pearls are valued for their luster and perfection of form. Brides traditionally wear a strand of white pearls, representing innocence and purity. With contemporary culture's disregard for this virtue, purity may be today's pearl of great price. As you blossom into womanhood, may you cultivate your femininity. May you prize your purity, shunning any influence that would taint you in mind or action. Your father and I pray for you daily and for the boy who may someday be your husband. May you save your physical love, so that, should marriage be in God's design for you, the strand of pearls encircling your neck on your wedding day will represent an imminent, sanctified union.

I would give you sapphires for beauty. Sapphires are valued for their beauty of color—a deep azure blue. May you walk in beauty carrying yourself with dignity and grace. May you live in beauty—an ordered life reinforced by custom and ceremony. May you respond to beauty wherever it be found: in the wonders of the natural world, in human artistic contributions, in noble deed or in the humble being of others.

I would give you opals for inner beauty. Opals are valued for their brilliant flashes of internal colors. "The king's daughter is all glorious within," sang the psalmist (Ps. 45:13 KJV). May your life radiate a beauty that finds its sources from the deep inner virtues summarized in Galatians 5: love that gives and receives . . . joy that fills your life with laughter and festivity . . . peace that passes understanding . . . patience that tolerates weakness . . . kindness that is tough and tender . . . self-control in action

221

and in thought ... goodness that delights in right ... faithfulness to God and neighbor ... a gentle spirit. .

Kimberly, for thirteen years you have graced our lives with your loving ways and gentle spirit. You have demonstrated these quiet traits in remarkable measure. You are sure to grow more lovely as you continue to cultivate that beauty from within.

When I was a teenager, my mother tucked a poem into the frame of my dresser mirror. As I prepared myself for a date with your father, it reminded me of a deeper and more lasting beauty:

> King's daughter!
>     Wouldst thou be all fair,
> Without—within—
>     Peerless and beautiful,
> A very Queen?
>     Know then:
> Not as men build unto the Silent One,—
>     With clang and clamour,
> Traffic of rude voices,
>     Clink of steel on stone,
> A Holy Place,
>     A place unseen,
> Each stone a prayer,
>     Then, having built
> Thy shrine sweep bare
>     Of self and sin,
> And all that might demean;
>     And, with endeavour,
> Watching ever, praying ever,
>     Keep it fragrant sweet and clean;
> So, by God's grace, it be fit place—

# AN OPEN LETTER TO KIMBERLY

His Christ shall enter and shall dwell therein.
Not as is earthly fame—where chase
   Of steel on stone may strive to win
Some outward grace,
   *Thy temple face is chiselled from within.*

—John Oxenham

Costly gems and precious metals are the inheritance of royalty. You have a yet greater inheritance that will never perish, spoil or fade, kept for you in heaven. Remember, dear, you are a daughter of *the* King!

Happy thirteenth birthday.

Lovingly,

Mother

## YOUR STORY

1. What character traits do you desire most for your children?
2. What are you doing to foster these qualities in your children?
3. What factors seriously threaten the development of strong character in your children?
4. How can you take advantage of transitions in your child's life to underscore important values?

# THE BIRDS AND THE BEES
## PREPARATION FOR SEXUAL MORALITY

"Jonathan thinks Dad's getting ready to tell him the facts of life," David confides with a twinkle in his eye.

"What gave him that idea?" I ask.

"I'm not sure. He said something about a book Dad gave him."

"That's funny. Dad never mentioned anything to me." Jonathan enters the room.

"What book did Dad give you?" I inquire.

"Oh, you know, the yellow one with flowers and butterflies on it. I think he's going to tell me the facts of life."

"What makes you think that?"

"Cause the book is all about flowers and butterflies, and it says it's a 'tale about *life*,' so I figured Dad was getting me ready for my talk."

"Do you know what the 'facts of life' are about?" I pursue.

"Not really. I just know you had talks with David and Kimberly about 'life,' and that's what the book's about," he answers with patient logic.

"Would you like Dad to tell you the facts of life?" I persist.

"It doesn't matter."

"Actually, the book Dad gave you is a story about caterpillars becoming butterflies, but we do have a good book about how you became a baby. Would you like me to get it for you?"

"Not now. I want to play basketball," he adds.

Watching Jonathan go out the back door, I wonder when we should have our talk with him. How much does he know? He doesn't seem all that interested, but we want to talk with him about human sexuality before someone else does. On the other hand, I don't want to burden him with knowledge he is not ready to handle.

I think back over our talks with David and Kimberly. One day without premeditation, Dave took David to Howard Johnson's and told all! I, in typical contrast, made detailed preparations to set a context and create an event for Kimberly's introduction to "life." With my Concordia text *Wonderfully Made* in hand, I headed with Kimberly to Bok Tower Gardens, where I selected an iron bench in a remote area. "After the story we'll get a sundae at the Garden Cafe," I promised her. Patiently she listened as I read the first section, "Love Brought You to Life." I advanced from "A Mother's Sex Organs" to "A Father's Sex Organs."

"Mom, why don't we stop right here," Kimberly suggested. "This part is about *boys*. We don't need to read about *them*. So why don't we just go get our sundaes?!"

I studied her uplifted face. Clearly the only thing on her mind was ice cream. Defeated, I departed for the cafe. Mission incomplete!

Six months later (following an incriminating moment at the dinner table when Kimberly astounded a dinner guest with the question, "What's a virgin?") I tried again. After a church sponsored "sex seminar" for junior-high girls at our home, I invited Kimberly to join me for our private viewing of the Concordia filmstrip *Take the High Road.* This time, in contrast to her previous indifference, Kimberly was full of questions. After more than an hour of discussion, Kimberly suddenly assumed a knowing look. "This was what you were trying to tell me at Bok Tower Gardens, wasn't it?"

I nodded and she continued, "I guess I just wasn't ready then."

I consider Jonathan in light of our approach to David and Kimberly. We've responded to questions they raised throughout the years, and we've also enlisted two invaluable resources to elicit questions and ensure systematic instruction: Concordia's graded sex education series and James Dobson's *Preparation for Adolescence.* During the child's early elementary years we read together the first Concordia book, *I Wonder, I Wonder,* which introduces basic facts about bodies, gestation, and birth within the context of God's design for the family.

The second book, *Wonderfully Made,* written for grades four through six, goes into greater detail, imparting an accurate description of the biological function of each sex along with a healthy attitude toward the knowledge. As in Kimberly's case, reading this book with a child generally reveals the level of interest and knowledge, helping you determine the direction in which to proceed.

Sometime during sixth grade (ready or not!) we have our official "facts of life" talk during which we review previous information and introduce the concept of sexual appetite and intimacy within a moral context. After this talk we present a gift of Dr. Dobson's *Preparation for Adolescence,* a frank and reassuring handbook written for preteens. It presents basic facts and anticipates the social and moral challenges teens are certain to encounter. As children read this book in privacy, facts are clarified and generally the door is open for further discussions.

I don't know how interested Jonathan is in this important subject. His comments, however, encourage me to prepare the way for Dave's talk. Time flies. Jonathan's growing up: Today's discussion about "flowers and butterflies" soon will advance to "birds and bees." So we'd better be ready!

## YOUR STORY

1. How did you learn the facts of life? What can you learn from your experience to help you instruct your children?
2. In what ways are you encouraging an open and honest atmosphere for questions and discussion?
3. None of us can control the total environment of our children. We can, however, control *our* input. What specific plans do you have to provide your child with information on his or her sexuality?

# GROWING PAINS
## PREPARATION FOR RESPONSIBLE
## INDEPENDENCE

"I'll be all packed and ready for tomorrow. So can't I please go out tonight?" pleads Kimberly. "I wouldn't go to bed any earlier if I stayed home," she reasons.

"I'm sorry. I'm just going to have to say no," I answer with finality.

Crestfallen, Kimberly walks out of the room. I review the week's events to justify my decision: Kimberly's exhausting week at work camp was followed by a late night at Jonathan's district all-star game. She spent all day Tuesday with friends. Wednesday she enjoyed a full day at the beach. The last two nights we were up late with family friends. Now she presses for yet another late evening—the night before she leaves for Camp Sonshine. Arbitrary though it seems to Kimberly, I simply must draw the line.

Bolstered in my decision by sheer logic, I still experience the letdown feeling that invariably follows the battle over boundaries. The children have always tested the limits. In the early years they pushed for later bedtimes, no naps, more television, less work, larger allowances. Now David and Kimberly strain for later curfews, more activities, our money instead of their earnings, and greater freedom in general. Jonathan strains to keep up with his older siblings.

("How come I have to go to bed when everyone else is up having a good time?")

No, the children's resistance is not new. The difference now is *my* uncertainty. The issues were clear-cut for my young brood. Certain limits were essential for their safety, health, and emotional well-being. Now the boundaries are less clear. The adolescents' legitimate need for increasing independence is complicated by their continued need for guidance and a basic consideration of the family unit.

Actually, limiting Kimberly's social life this evening was a fairly easy decision based on schedule overload, not the particular activity. The issues we've faced with David this year have been more difficult: driving into Orlando at night without previous experience with city traffic; listening to "teenage music" in a room shared with a grade-school brother; open-ended evenings with buddies who have cars but no specific plans. Each issue requires separate consideration. Rarely is the solution clear-cut.

Testing the limits is not only natural to this stage; it is necessary. Adolescence marks a child's transition from an inherited morality (observed because parents say it is best) to a personal morality (observed because the child believes it is best). Resistance or even rebellion is inevitable as teenagers examine and evaluate the basis for their parents' decisions that contradict their own desires. Maturity is reached by painful but essential testing and sorting.

The challenge for us parents is to keep open the lines of communication so that even as teens chafe against the boundaries, they experience our understanding and support. When Dave and I take the time to explain our reasoning—and even the uncertainty—behind our decisions, the children seem to benefit.

Actually, we've had minimal stress during these poten-

tially difficult years because of two guiding principles culled
from writings and observation of others more experienced
than ourselves. The first, our limited-options theory, is
based on the belief that it is easier to ease than tighten
controls. In practice, we start with limited options, gradually increasing the options with age and with evidence of
dependability. This keeps parents in the position of control
and casts them more frequently as the "good guys" who
dispense rather than deny privileges. This position offers us
bargaining power: added privileges for demonstration of
added dependability. Even the pain of restriction is eased as
we anticipate with the frustrated child specific liberties at
definite dates. (David's disappointment at not having unlim-
ited access to the car was mollified when we shared goals of
granting him greater independence in his senior year.)

The second principle provides an important balance to
the first: Say yes whenever possible; save no for essentials.
This distinguishes the important from the unimportant and
checks an unfortunate negativism acquired during early
years of parenting. ("No, no!" "Don't touch!") The administration of Bok Tower Gardens has recognized the effect of
the affirmative, insisting that all signs be cast in the positive:
"Please leave your pets in the car," rather than, "Pets not
permitted"; "Visitors required to wear shoes," rather than,
"Bare feet not allowed." A general yes posture creates a
better climate for the occasional, necessary no.

Dave and I want to do everything in our power to be
allies of our teenagers, helping them through these predict-
ably stressful transitional years. To this end James Dobson
urges a conversation with the adolescent in which the parent
prepares him or her for the strain placed on the family
during the process of growing up and becoming responsible

for one's own life. He suggests that parents conclude this conversation with the following commitments:

(1) I am going to give you a little more freedom each year, as I think you are ready for it. There will be certain things that you will have to accept as long as you are living at home and you will not always like the rules that are established here. However, your mother and I will gradually allow you to make more of your own decisions as you grow older.

(2) As your freedom increases, so will your level of responsibility. I'll expect you to carry more and more of the family work load, and you'll earn a greater percentage of your own spending money. This responsibility will help prepare you for successful adult living.

(3) If you ever feel we are being unfair with you during the teenage years, you are free to come to us and express your feelings. You can say what you really think, and I'll consider your viewpoint. However, I will never honor a temper tantrum. If you slam doors and pout and scream, as many teenagers do when they get upset, you'll find my ears completely closed.

(4) Above all, remember that you are tremendously loved, and everything that we do will be motivated by that affection. And even if we get upset with each other in the years to come, that deep love will always be there. Before we know it, you'll be gone and we'll only have memories of

231

these happy days together. Let's make the most of them as a family.[6]

Conflict is a major growing pain of adolescence—for teenagers and their parents. But with sensitivity, effort, and prayer, these pressure-filled years can be a stimulating and stretching adventure leading to a loving relationship with our adult children!

## YOUR STORY

1. In what areas are your children testing their limits? What outside pressures compound this problem?
2. What is your reaction to their resistance? What should it be?
3. In setting limits, what areas give you the greatest uncertainty? What can you do to deal more effectively with these areas?
4. Why is resistance a normal, healthy aspect of growing up?

# LEAD THEM SAFELY HOME
# PREPARATION FOR PARENTAL RELEASE

All is quiet at home. Dave and the younger children have gone to bed. I keep vigil until David's return. The sound of rain distracts me from my reading. 11:45 P.M. David should be on the highway now. Is it raining in Winter Haven? Has David ever driven in rain? Does he know how to work the brakes on slippery roads?

I begin to review possible perils between Winter Haven and home: the foggy dark, slick roads, dangerous intersections, drunk drivers. David is a responsible kid, but he's young. His judgment is limited by inexperience. Is he ready for such adult responsibility?

A familiar wave of anxiety washes over me as I multiply my present concern times all imaginable risks of the adolescent years. Newspaper and periodicals relentlessly record the perils of youth: drug abuse, illicit sex, stress, suicide. . . . From his early childhood we have trained and instructed David in our value system. We've tried to prepare him for the challenges of society. But is he prepared to stand up to these challenges? Is he ready for increasing involvement in the world beyond our direct supervision?

Am *I* ready? How does a parent survive these risk-filled years when a teenager is no longer a child but not yet an adult? How does one increasingly release an adolescent to an uncertain world without becoming immobilized with fear? What assurances can the parent of an adolescent claim? Where can one turn for guidance?

Are ancient biblical principles and promises applicable to twentieth-century society? Society changes along with its specific problems, but concern for your young never changes. Nor does the time-proven approach for facing those worries.

The consistent teaching of Scripture concerning anxiety is clearly stated in Paul's letter to the Philippians: "Do not be anxious about anything, but in everything, by prayer and petition, with thanksgiving, present your requests to God. And the peace of God, which transcends all understanding, will guard your hearts and your minds in Christ Jesus" (4:6–7). Simply stated, *our* work is to release our worries with an act of prayer; *God's* work is to guard our hearts and minds with His peace.

Properly channeled, anxiety can serve a useful purpose. Just as physical pain often indicates a problem requiring medical attention, emotional discomfort can indicate a problem requiring spiritual attention. Our spirit-aches can act as nerve endings, reminders to pray. Concern for our children is a given in this uncertain world. Each time we are assailed with anxiety, we must choose: to nourish worry by dwelling on real or imagined possibilities or to turn each worry into prayer. When we convert anxiety into prayer, we exchange it for God's peace—peace that "transcends all understanding." We turn to God—the only safe place.

Can we be certain our prayers will guarantee our children's physical safety? Not necessarily. Our confidence comes not from the particular answers to our prayers but from the One to whom we pray. We can be sure, however, that God cares more perfectly than we about our children's welfare. Nothing will touch them that has not first passed through the filter of His love.

One of my favorite insights into God's loving protection is from C. S. Lewis's fifth chronicle of Narnia, *The Horse and His Boy*. This story relates the adventures of Bree, a talking horse, and his boy, Shasta, as they embark on a mission to save Narnia from enemy invasion. Throughout their perilous journey they are plagued by encounters with lions. During a dangerous night journey over a steep mountain pass, Shasta discovers he is accompanied by yet another lion. This time the lion speaks, revealing that the many lions Shasta has feared were actually one.

> I was the lion who forced you to join with Aravis. I was the cat who comforted you among the houses of the dead. I was the lion who drove the jackals from you while you slept. I was the lion who gave the Horses the new strength of fear for the last mile so that you should reach King Lune in time. And I was the lion you do not remember who pushed the boat in which you lay, a child near death, so that it came to shore where a man sat, wakeful at midnight, to receive you.[7]

Aslan, the Christ-figure, had accompanied Shasta throughout his mission, becoming whatever Shasta needed to get safely "home." As we continually "present our requests to God," He acts. Regardless of outcome, God will be present, guarding our "hearts and minds in Christ Jesus."

A prayer from the *Book of Common Prayer,* cross-stitched and matted, is propped against a window in the morning room. Each morning when I open the curtains, I am greeted by these words of commitment and release: "O God, we entrust all who are dear to us to thy never-failing care and love, for this life and the life to come; knowing that thou art doing for them better things than we can desire or pray for."

Even as I release to God immediate concerns for my loved ones, I am reminded of His loving concern for their safety, physical and spiritual, now and for eternity.

So I pray that David will return home safely tonight. And I pray that he will be led home each day in the safety of the Father's love.

## YOUR STORY

1. What are your greatest anxieties for your children? Over which of these concerns do you have control? Over which do you *not* have control?
2. What is the role of prayer in relation to your fears?
3. What does it mean to release your child to God's care? Do you trust God with the care of your children?

# ALL OTHER GROUND
# PREPARATION FOR A PERSONAL FAITH

Summer vacation is drawing to a close. Two more days before we pack our suitcases and leave my parents' home to return to Lake Wales and the first day of a new school year—David's last year at home. Even as I sit alone at the Corner Restaurant fortified by a stack of reading materials and a steaming mug of coffee, David is experiencing his first in a series of interviews with prospective colleges.

David's last year at home. All year long the mail has brought brochures from colleges throughout the country. David has faithfully checked the entrance requirements for the schools that interested him. He has registered for the Scholastic Achievement Test and selected senior courses for the college-bound student. But nothing has brought home the wrenching reality of our limited time with David quite like this first college interview.

The thought of this self-sufficient young man making his independent journey to the college admissions office triggers a flood of memories of other "firsts" he has pioneered in our family. As if it were yesterday I remember bundling him in a blue blanket for his first journey from the hospital to our home. How Dave and I studied his every move during those early months, marveling over each new

CHAPTER 7

development: his eyes following the mobile dangling over his crib, his rolling over, his scooting about the floor on all-fours. . . . Each accomplishment was faithfully recorded in his baby book: first words, drinking with a cup, putting words into phrases and phrases into sentences, being completely toilet trained. His status changed to "big brother" and the records became sketchy as we struggled to accommodate new babies into a family unit, all the time David leading the way—first day at school, first Little League game, first week at camp, first license, first date—teaching us as we guided him.

So now, once again, David leads the way, but this time with a giant step—a flying leap away from home. My musings go beyond sentiment to the enormity of this next transition. The break from home to college will significantly influence other critical life decisions: his academic major, his vocation, maybe his life partner! All these decisions will be made apart from our direct supervision.

Will he be ready? Have we adequately trained him in skills requisite for independent living? Have we schooled him sufficiently in the fundamentals of the faith? Will he be faithful to his Christian heritage? I consider the warning of James Dobson as he ponders the biblical account of devoted Samuel's ungodly children: "The message is loud and clear to me: God will not necessarily save our children as a reward for our own devotion! Christianity is not inherited by the next generation. We must do our early homework, if we are to be successful in this vital responsibility."[8]

Have we done our homework? I review our efforts to train David in the way he should go. Surely, the church program has provided a solid scriptural background. We likewise have attempted to be regular in our systematic Bible reading and prayer. Doubtless, however, the bulk of his learning has transpired spontaneously in the life laboratory, home, as we approached together the tasks, conflicts, disciplines, values, choices, and transitions implicit in daily living. Donald Joy has said that "fathers and mothers, just in the business of doing their parenting, are unwittingly the first curriculum for representing God."[9] What kind of "curriculum" have we provided for David through the years? Have we offered a model of a viable lifestyle for him? Most important, has the overall teaching and training led him into a vital relationship with Christ, the rock of our faith?

Even as I examine our endeavors to train and nurture David, I recognize our limitations. We provide whatever instruction we can, but the response is up to him. Regardless of the strength or weakness of our approach—cajole, persuade, intimidate—the Spirit of God alone can convince; David alone can respond. And in this recognition comes release. Whether at home under our watchful supervision or one thousand miles away at the school of his choice, David is ultimately accountable to God, not to us. David is God's child, not ours. We are temporary stewards of this tremendous trust but not owners. We will be forced by distance to do what we as stewards have been commanded to do all along: release him to the care of his heavenly Father.

This act of release brings a great sense of liberation. In truth, the total responsibility for raising our children has never been ours alone. Even as we have strived to instruct, train, and provide a nourishing home environment, there have been countless others who have richly contributed to their lives. Siblings, extended family, friends, caring teachers, coaches, as well as life's varied experiences, all are instruments used by God in the stretching and shaping of children. Is there any reason to fear that God will stop working in David's life when he is out of our sight?

Christ provides for parents a beautiful example of release as He prayed for His disciples before His return to His heavenly home. "Holy Father, protect them by the power of your name," He prayed. With parental concern He continued, "While I was with them, I protected them and kept them safe." Stating His desire that they might have the "full measure" of His joy, He concluded His prayer with two petitions toward that end: "My prayer is not that you take them out of the world but that you protect them from the evil one. . . . Sanctify them by the truth; your word is truth" (John 17:11–12, 15, 17).

Dr. Kenneth Kantzer, addressing the issue of building faith in children, has stated, ". . . our goal is not to instruct them precisely in what we know to be right, but to enable them to become self-instructing persons who make their own decisions in the light of the Word of God."[10] As I anticipate David's departure for college, I can pray with confidence Christ's prayer of release: Protect him from evil forces while he is strengthened and edified by truth as defined in God's Word.

I am not indifferent to the challenges ahead in David's last year at home. I will most certainly avail myself of every opportunity to reinforce the Christian values upon which Dave and I have based our lives. But in reality, the bulk of our training has transpired. Now, at last, we can only hope to guide David as he continues to gain experience in the maturing process of making decisions.

There is no greater security for our children than to release them to Christ, the solid Rock, the very foundation of our faith. In the words of hymn writer Edward Mote, "All other ground is sinking sand." I pray for the trust to

ALL OTHER GROUND

release my children as He did His disciples into the loving
care of our heavenly Father.

### For Our Children

Father, hear us, we are praying,
  Hear the words our hearts are saying,
We are praying for our children.
  Keep them from the powers of evil.
From the secret, hidden peril,
  From the whirlpool that would suck them,
From the treacherous quicksand, pluck them.

From the worldling's hollow gladness,
  From the sting of faithless sadness,
Holy Father, save our children.

Through life's troubled waters steer them,
  Through life's bitter battle cheer them,
Father, Father, be Thou near them.
  Read the language of our longing,
Read the wordless pleadings thronging,
  Holy Father, for our children.

*And wherever they may bide,
  Lead them Home at eventide.*[11]

## YOUR STORY

1. What kind of "curriculum" in the Christian faith are
you providing within the home? What kind of
Christian nurture or support are your children getting
outside the home?

2. What is the difference between teaching and training your children? What are you doing to train your children in the teachings of your faith?
3. How does the realization that you are the stewards, not owners, of God's children affect your view of parenting?
4. Why does a personal relationship with Christ provide the greatest security for your children throughout life?

# EPILOGUE

# LAND OF HEART'S DESIRE

*But trailing clouds of glory
    do we come
From God, who is our home.*
            —*William Worsdsworth*

Rounding the corner, I pull the car into our driveway. Light beams a welcome from windows shimmering in the night. Gazing through the clear glass, I feel an unexpected surge of joy. Oh, the comforting presence of home! A snug ship anchored in a sheltering harbor.

How I wish I could keep my family forever safe in this protective place. How I crave reassurance that my domestic efforts will guarantee immunity from threat or harm. I'm not alone in my desire. The Germans have a word, almost untranslatable, that expresses this desired state of total peace, *geborgenheit:* "the feeling of being surrounded and protected as if by one's mother's arm." Our efforts to create a home are in part an attempt to create such an environment. Yet often our best efforts seem poor protection from life's evils. And, strangely, at moments of greatest happiness we experience vague yearnings for something more.

Pascal, in his classic *Pensées,* acknowledged a universal longing for something other, something more, and calls it nostalgia. C. S. Lewis referred to a lifelong nostalgia: "our longing to be reunited with something in the universe from which we now feel cut off, to be on the inside of some door which we have always seen from the outside."[1]

245

# EPILOGUE

What is this place that all people see, consciously or unconsciously? Paul Tournier, in his probing book *A Place for You,* answered,

> I believe it is the place of perfection, which in fact does not exist in this world—a place that will give real security and protection from disappointment. It is our homesickness for Paradise. The place we are all looking for is the Paradise we have lost. The whole of humanity suffers from what we might call "The Paradise Lost Complex."[2]

Lewis insisted that this nostalgia is no neurotic fancy but "the true index of our real situation."[3]

What then is our "real situation"? Scripture speaks directly to this question, clarifying our status as "aliens and strangers in the world" (1 Peter 2:11). In the New Testament Abraham is held up as an example of one who understood his position. Without a backward glance he left his familiar securities for an unknown land because "he was looking forward to the city with foundations, whose architect and builder is God" (Heb. 11:10). Indeed, all who are listed in the scriptural Hall of Fame "admitted that they were aliens and strangers on earth . . . They were longing for a better country—a heavenly one" (Heb 11:13, 16).

There are those pilgrim souls, those saints, who just seem to know, like Abraham, the relative insignificance of earthly places in light of their eternal home. They hold lightly things of this earth because they have a strong sense of their citizenship in heaven. Others gain this perspective when their earthly supports are found to be inadequate. The spiritual "This world is not my home, I'm just a-passing through" was the heartfelt song of the slaves for whom

246

heaven was the only certain place of their own. *Pilgrim's Progress,* John Bunyan's amazing allegory of Christian's pilgrimage to the celestial city, was written in the void of prison.

But most of us, like myself, are earthbound. We build our habitats and settle in as if they were permanent houses.

It was Christ who clarified our true situation when He left His heavenly home to dwell among us for a brief sojourn. As His days on earth came to an end, He gathered His disciples around Himself to prepare them for His departure. Tenderly He said, "Do not let your hearts be troubled" (John 14:1), explaining that He was going to prepare a place for them, a *home*—a perfect dwelling where "there will be no more death or mourning or crying or pain" (Rev. 21:4). Paradise. "The Land of Heart's Desire."

But He did not leave them alone, orphans with only hearts full of memories and heads full of dreams. No. He promised to send a "Comforter," the Holy Spirit who would reside in their hearts. He would make His home *within* all believers—a present comfort plus a form of earnest, a guarantee on our future, permanent, and perfect home.

So what do we conclude? Do we set aside our building manuals, cancel activity on construction sites? Of course not. The more closely we build our homes to the master Architect's specifications, the more fully we experience in the present the heavenly happiness and security we anticipate. We continue to build our homes, attending to the details that nourish and edify family, friends, and strangers. But we do so recognizing the limitations of our endeavors. We view it from an eternal perspective:

# EPILOGUE

The settled happiness and security which we all desire, God withholds from us by the very nature of the world: but joy, pleasure, and merriment, He has scattered broadcast. We are never safe, but we have plenty of fun, and some ecstasy. It is not hard to see why. The security we crave would teach us to rest our hearts in this world and oppose an obstacle to our return to God: A few moments of happy love, a landscape, a symphony, a merry meeting with our friends, a bath or a football match, have no such tendency. Our Father refreshes us on the journey with some pleasant inns, but will not encourage us to mistake them for home.[4]

As sojourners we pause from time to time, refreshing ourselves at some pleasant inns. But pain is mingled with our pleasure and sorrow with our joy. Irrepressible longings remind us of something better: heaven, "The Land of Heart's Desire," and God, "who is our Home."

How vast the treasure we possess!
   How rich Thy bounty, King of grace!
This world is ours, and worlds to come;
   Earth is our lodge, and heaven our home. . . .
I would not change my blest estate
   For all the world calls good or great.
—Isaac Watts

# NOTES

## Prologue

1. Quoted in Frank Trippett, "Why There Is No Place Like It," *Time* (November 29, 1982), 100.
2. Elizabeth Goudge, *Joy of the Snow* (New York: Coward, McCann and Geoghegan), 126.

## Chapter 1: Foundations: "Build Sure in the Beginning"

1. W. B. Yeats, "A Prayer for My Daughter," *The Collected Poems of W. B. Yeats* (New York: Macmillan, 1956), 186.
2. Quoted in Seamus Heaney, *Preoccupations* (New York: Farrar, Straus, & Giroux, 1980), 139–40.
3. *Funk and Wagnalls Standard Primer* (New York: Funk and Wagnalls, 1947), 69.
4. Marjorie Kinnan Rawlings, *Cross Creek* (New York: Scribner's, 1942), 3.
5. Robert Blanding, *Floridays* (New York: Dodd, Mead, 1941), 19.
6. Quoted in Douglas Gilbert & Clyde Kilby, *C. S. Lewis: Images of His World* (Grand Rapids: Eerdmans, 1973), 77.
7. Rawlings, *Cross Creek*, 3.
8. Anne Morrow Lindbergh, *The Flower and the Nettle* (New York: Harcourt Brace Jovanovich, 1976), 295.
9. Robert Johnson, *She: Understanding Feminine Psychology* (New York: Harper & Row, 1976), 45.

10. C. S. Lewis, *A Preface to Paradise Lost* (New York: Oxford, 1961), 17.

11. Thomas Howard, *Splendor in the Ordinary* (Wheaton, Ill.: Tyndale House, 1976), 68.

12. Alexandra Stoddard, *Living a Beautiful Life* (New York: Random House, 1986), 4–5.

13. Quoted in Gaston Bachelard, *The Poetics of Space* (Boston: Beacon Press, 1969), 54.

14. Dietrich Bonhoeffer, *Letters and Papers from Prison* (New York: Macmillan, 1972), 165.

15. Ibid., 235.

16. Ibid., 207.

17. C. S. Lewis, *Surprised by Joy* (New York: Harcourt, Brace and World, 1955), 177.

18. James Dobson, *Straight Talk to Men and Their Wives* (Waco, Tex.: Word Books, 1984).

## Chapter 2: Roof and Exterior Walls: Sheltering Elements

1. Michael Novak. (Despite my diligent pursuits, I haven't pinned down the source of this quote. Forgive me, Mr. Novak.)

2. Elie Wiesel, *Night* (New York: Farrar, Straus & Giroux), 93.

3. Frank Lloyd Wright, *A Testament* (New York: Horizon Press, 1957).

4. David Lowry, *The Cranbrook Journal* (May 1984).

5. Quoted in Isabel Anders, "The Grace of Courtesy," *Eternity* (March 1986), 26.

6. M. Scott Peck, *The Road Less Traveled* (New York: Simon and Schuster, 1978), 127–28.

7. James Dobson, "The Importance of Family Traditions," *A Christmas Sampler from the Dobsons* (Pomona, Calif.: Focus on the Family), n.p.

# NOTES

8. Haddon Robinson, *Grief* (Christian Medical Society, 1976), 21.

## Chapter 3: Walls: Delineation of Space and Place

1. Thomas Howard, *Splendor in the Ordinary* (Wheaton, Ill.: Tyndale House, 1976), 35.
2. Quoted in Christian Norberg-Schulz, *The Concept of Dwelling* (New York: Rizzoli, 1985), 102.
3. Ibid., 111.
4. Ibid., 105.
5. Thomas Frederick Davies, *The Diversion of Staying Home* (Dutton, 1935), 24.
6. Mary Ellen Chase, *The White Gate* (New York: Norton, 1954), 179.
7. Elisabeth Elliot, *Discipline: The Glad Surrender* (Old Tappan, N.J.: Revell, 1982), 130.
8. Gaston Bachelard, *The Poetics of Space* (Boston: Beacon Press, 1969), 65.
9. Mark Hampton, *On Decorating* (New York: Random House, 1989), 91.
10. Georg Anderson, *Interior Decorating* (Minneapolis: Bethany House, 1983), 37.
11. JoAnn Barwick, "Thinking Aloud," *House Beautiful* (June 1982), 8.
12. Hampton, *On Decorating*, 173.
13. Ibid., 82.
14. Attributed to Louis Evans, Sr.

## Chapter 4: Elements of Style: Decoration and Design

1. Russell Lynes, "Leisure and Style," *Architectural Digest* (November 1984), 84.
2. *The Saarinen Door: Eliel Saarinen, Architect and Designer*

*at Cranbrook* (Bloomfield Hills, Mich.: Cranbrook Academy, 1963), 59.

3. William Strunk, *The Elements of Style* (New York: Macmillan, 1979), 84.

4. Frank Lloyd Wright, *A Testament* (New York: Horizon, 1957), 228.

5. Barbara Lazear Ascher, "A Personal Tradition," *House & Garden* (February 1984), 76.

6. Decorating Editors of McCall's, *McCall's Decorating Book* (New York: Random House, 1964), xi.

7. Edith Schaeffer, *Hidden Art* (Wheaton, Ill.: Tyndale House, 1971), 76–77.

8. Lesley Blanch, *Architectural Digest* (September 1985), 34.

9. Quoted in Ascher, "Personal Tradition," *House & Garden* (February 1984), 82.

10. Quoted in Michael Mott, *The Seven Mountains of Thomas Merton* (New York: Houghton Mifflin, 1984), 6.

11. *Design in America* (New York: Harry N. Abrams, 1983), 26.

12. Dee Hardie, *Hollyhocks, Lambs and Other Passions* (New York: Atheneum, 1985), 146.

13. Dorothy Rodgers, *My Favorite Things* (New York: Atheneum, 1964), 69.

14. Ibid.

15. Gaston Bachelard, *The Poetics of Space* (Boston: Beacon Press, 1969), 68.

16. Dietrich Bonhoeffer, *Letters and Papers from Prison* (New York: Macmillan, 1972), 168.

## Chapter 5: Doors and Thresholds: The Open Door of Hospitality

1. "Secrets to Grace, Charm, and That Old South Style," *House Beautiful* (March 1982), 19.

# NOTES

2. Quoted in Georg Anderson, *Interior Decorating* (Minneapolis: Bethany House, 1983), 89.

3. Henri Nouwen, *Reaching Out* (Garden City: Doubleday, 1975), 51.

4. Karen Mains, *Open Heart, Open Home* (Elgin, Ill.: David C. Cook, 1976), 28.

5. Mains, *Open Heart, Open Home,* 25.

6. Nouwen, *Reaching Out,* 73.

7. Ibid., 56.

8. Ibid.

9. Kenneth MacLeod, "Rune of Hospitality," *A Modern Book of Hours,* Helena F. Olton, ed. (Norwich, Conn.: C. R. Gibson, 1973), 34.


## Chapter 6: Window-Songs: A Personal View

1. Robert Johnson, *She* (New York: Harper & Row, 1976), 59.

2. Lee Hall, "Life and Letters," *House & Garden* (October 1983), 10.

3. Rumer Godden, *The Kitchen Madonna* (New York: Viking Press, 1966), 21.

4. Available from Scripture Union, 7000 Ludlow Street, Upper Darby, PA 19082.


## Chapter 7: The Road by My Door: Growing Up to Go Away

1. Howard H. Callaway, *The Story of a Man and a Garden* (Princeton, N.J.: Princeton Univ. Press, 1965), 11.

2. Erik Erickson, *Childhood and Society* (New York: Hawthorne, 1964), 16.

3. Lilias Trotter, *Parables of the Cross* (London: Marshall Brothers, n.d.), 5.

# NOTES

4. Virginia Stem Owens, "The Necessity of Death," *Christianity Today* (April 6, 1984), 19.

5. W. B. Yeats, "A Cradle Song," *The Collected Poems of W. B. Yeats* (New York: Macmillan, 1956), 39.

6. James Dobson, *Hide or Seek* (Old Tappan, N.J.: Revell, 1974), 124–25.

7. C. S. Lewis, *The Horse and His Boy* (New York: Macmillan, 1954), paperback, 158.

8. James Dobson, *A Checklist for Spiritual Training* (Arcadia, Calif.: Focus on the Family, 1982), 1.

9. Donald Joy, "Building Faith: How a Child Learns to Love God," *Christianity Today* (June 13, 1986), 4–1.

10. Kenneth Kantzer, "Final Thoughts," *Christianity Today* (June 13, 1986), 16–1.

11. Amy Carmichael, "For Our Children," *Toward Jerusalem* (Fort Washington, Pa.: Christian Literature Crusade, n.d.), 106.

## Epilogue

1. C. S. Lewis, *The Weight of Glory and Other Addresses* (New York: Macmillan, 1975), 16.

2. Paul Tournier, *A Place for You* (New York: Harper & Row, 1968), 37.

3. Lewis, *The Weight of Glory*, 16.

4. C. S. Lewis, *The Problem of Pain* (New York: Macmillan, 1962), 115.

4